THE DEVIL
COMES TO
DARTMOOR

'I'd rather walk a hundred miles,
And run by night and day,
Than have that carriage halt for me
And hear my ladye say –
'Now pray step in, and make no din,
Step in with me to ride;
There's room, I trow, by me for you,
And all the world beside.'
Sabine Baring-Gould, 1908

THE DEVIL COMES TO DARTMOOR

THE HAUNTING TRUE STORY OF
MARY HOWARD
DEVON'S 'DEMON BRIDE'

LAURA QUIGLEY

For Bette
A great lady
A generous soul
May she enjoy the rest of her journey

First published 2011

The History Press
The Mill, Brimscombe Port
Stroud, Gloucestershire, GL5 2QG
www.thehistorypress.co.uk

British Library Cataloguing in Publication Data.
A catalogue record for this book is available from the British Library.

ISBN 978 0 7524 6111 3

Typesetting and origination by The History Press
Printed in Great Britain
Manufacturing managed by Jellyfish Print Solutions Ltd

CONTENTS

Notes on the Text   6
Acknowledgements   9
Principle Characters and Locations   11

 1 A Tale of Three Fathers   13
 2 The Terror Begins   35
 3 Revenge Served Cold   54
 4 An Heir Apparent   66
 5 The Devil Comes to Dartmoor   80
 6 A Marriage Under Fire   90
 7 Declarations of War   107
 8 Triumph of a Traitor   126
 9 A Fool and His Money   145
10 A Man of Means   156
11 A Spirited Lady   179

Timeline   190
Family Trees:
The Courtenays of Powderham   197
The Cutteford and Halse Families   198
The Grenville Family   199
The Howard Family of Saffron Walden   200
References   201

Notes on the Text

The seventeenth century was a turbulent era in European history, a time of global exploration, epidemics and, it seems, perpetual conflict. In Britain in the 1640s, there were a series of very well-documented battles which are collectively called the 'English Civil War' and I, like most others, have retained this name for clarity. However, these wars destroyed lives across Scotland, Wales, Ireland, England and parts of France, and imported mercenaries from all over Europe. Thousands of Scots were killed or enslaved and sent to the New World in the midst of this English Civil War, and the brutal events did not end with the execution of King Charles I. Their impact was felt across Britain and Ireland and into Europe for many years, and I am sorry not to be able to present more of the story in this book. I have concentrated here on characters in Devon and must leave those other stories for better writers and scholars than I.

It could be argued that this English Civil War was led by opposing factions in London, the English gentry battling amongst themselves for supremacy; it was 'English' in that sense, but if ever a war was incorrectly named, this one was. Some historians are now referring to these wars as the 'British Civil Wars' or the 'Wars of the Three Kingdoms', titles which are perhaps more appropriate, but the term 'English Civil War' still predominates, so I use it here merely for continuity.

The calendar year used to start in March, so, like many writers, I have amended some year dates for a modern audience, and to maintain a consistency with other histories.

For example, January 1643 in their calendar is translated to January 1644 in ours, while dates from April to December remain unchanged.

England in the early seventeenth century was a very different country, before de-regulation of the markets, before universal suffrage, before national health care systems, and before law and order was systematically co-ordinated. Corruption was expected, land ownership was the signifier of success, and religion was an essential aspect – some might even say the defining characteristic – of any community. Yet in exploring the lives of the people of seventeenth-century Devon, I have been surprised and at times shocked by their modern attitudes and thinking, by the similarities with modern-day Britain, by the ideas they conceived, thoughts would still be influencing the world some 400 years later.

Essentially this book is a love story, and like all great love stories, I make no apologies for the characters' flaws. They were human beings just like us, often overwhelmed by emotions and ambitions, trying to do their best in a world that was descending into madness.

Acknowledgements

My sincere thanks go to my parents for reading early versions of this book and offering corrections and encouragement. The research started as a play called *The Advocate* which was first performed as a public reading in London, for Amnesty International – thanks to all the cast and production team who made that possible. And I must thank my friend Lisa Tetley for all her wonderful, generous support for both the play and the book over all this time. Many others have also contributed and offered their support over the years, including, in no particular order: Ade Morris; Andrew Smaje; Mike Kaloski-Naylor; Ben Mitchell; Angela Sherlock; Danny Reilly; Colin Archer; David Lane; Robert Chapman and Dr Tom Greeves. Dr Greeves gave me some wonderful feedback on an early draft.

My family have had to support me through some difficult times over such an extended period, so huge thanks to them, and thanks to all those who so graciously contributed photographs and images. The Archive Staff at the Inns of Court; Plymouth and West Devon Record Office; West Sussex Record Office and Devon Record Office were just wonderful. I am particularly grateful to all those who have explored the story before me, from Mrs G. Radford and Amos C. Miller for the Devonshire Association, to more recently Gerry Woodcock and Kevin Hynes. I hope I have remembered you all in the *References* section and given you the credit you deserve. I am also indebted to Cate Ludlow at the History Press for all her hard work and advice, and for believing in the project.

My final thanks goes to everyone who is researching their family and local histories – your efforts and contributions have maintained so many research services that otherwise might have failed for lack of funding, and have recently made available so much new material. It is both humbling and fascinating to be involved in such an enormous endeavour on the part of so many people. I am delighted to see communities preserving their own histories in a continuum of study, investigating why things are as they are now, and how things have changed. Remembering previous generations is so essential to understanding ourselves. The efforts of those individuals discovering, exploring and translating parish and other records, and making them available online for everyone to access should be celebrated – it is a terrific achievement and long may their generous and inspirational work continue.

I do hope that everyone enjoys the book, finished at last. All mistakes are my own and any comments and corrections are gratefully and graciously received.

My journey ends here.

Laura Quigley, 2011

Principle Characters and Locations

At Fitzford, Tavistock

Mary Fitz
Sir John Fitz and Bridget Courtenay (her parents)
Sir Alan Percy, Sir Thomas Darcy, Sir Charles Howard and the villain of the piece Sir Richard Grenville – her husbands
Mary Vernon (née Howard), Richard Grenville, and Elizabeth Lennard (née Grenville) – her children

At Walreddon, near Tavistock

George Cutteford, his wife Grace, and their children, George, John, Eleanor, Grace, and Anne
Richard Halse and his family
George Halse/Howard, son of Mary Fitz and George Cutteford (who became a ward of Sir Francis Trelawney of Venn)

At Powderham Castle, near Exmouth

Sir William Courtenay, Earl of Devon
Sir Francis Courtenay (his son)
Sir William Courtenay (his grandson)

At Audley End, Saffron Walden

Sir Thomas Howard, Earl of Suffolk
Theophilus Howard (his son), also living at Lulworth Castle
in Dorset
James Howard and George Howard (his grandsons)

In Oxford in 1644

King Charles I
Prince Charles, Prince of Wales; Prince James, Duke of York
(his sons)
Edward Sackville, Earl of Dorset, Lord Chamberlain to the
King (also with houses at Knole in Kent, and Withyham in
Dorset)
Sir John Maynard, once attorney to King Charles I

In Exeter, 1644

Sir John Berkeley, Royalist Governor of Exeter

Chapter One

A Tale of Three Fathers

Elizabeth I.

Mary Howard's ghost, it is said, haunts the heart of Dartmoor. Some say they have seen her spectral form at the gatehouse of her old home in Tavistock; others that they have glimpsed a mysterious coach travelling across the moors. The spectre of her dog, with demonic eyes, has been seen running along the dark lanes to Okehampton Castle. The stories have been told over and over in the old pubs in Tavistock and Okehampton, perhaps as a warning to unwary travellers or to hurry the drunks off home to bed. Even the famous lyricist and historian Sabine Baring-Gould[1] recalled a number of eyewitness accounts of the famous white lady who appears every night at midnight by the Tavistock gatehouse. There she boards a spectral coach made of human bones; the skulls of her four husbands are at each corner, and it is driven by a headless coachman.

---

1   Baring-Gould, 1908.

A skeletal black dog with fiery eyes accompanies her, running alongside the coach, as she rides across the winding roads of Dartmoor, past the ruins of old Lydford Gaol and out towards Okehampton. On arrival at Okehampton Castle, she plucks a blade of grass, and then rides back again, all the way back to that gatehouse, back and forth every night from midnight till dawn. She must make this same journey every night for eternity as penance for her sins, for murdering her four husbands, so they say, and when she has taken every blade of grass from Okehampton Castle, the world will end.[2]

If someone sees the white lady on the road, according to the legend, there will be a death. Perhaps there is some truth in that, as from the moment an attorney called George Cutteford met the young Mary Howard, his life would be marked by tragedy.

The story of Mary Howard and her attorney, however, starts many years before she was born, when, in 1582, a sailor called William Cutteford climbed the steps to an attorney's office on the Sutton Pool docks in Plymouth, to have his will written for him.[3]

A sailor's life in Elizabethan England was a precarious one. William Cutteford would have worked for hire on many different ships, perhaps for merchants or the navy, perhaps for the customs officers who regularly battled smugglers and pirates along the many harbours and inlets around the coast of southwest England. Sailors frequently died at sea, in accidents, in battle, or by disease. William Cutteford now had a family to

---

2   Some variations on the story say that Mary Howard must make her journey until the end of the world, or until every blade of grass has gone from Okehampton Park. I prefer the (probably more modern) version: when every blade of grass has gone from Okehampton Park, only then will the world end. The impossibility of removing every blade of grass means the world will never end, a message I personally prefer.

3   PROB 11/65, 'The will of William Cuttiford, mariner, of Plymouth, 15th February 1582' (or 1581 in the old calendar). Held at the National Archives, London. The surname is spelled Cuttiford throughout; it is likely George Cutteford changed the spelling when he signed on for work as a customs officer. However, to save confusion, I have standardised the spelling as Cutteford.

care for, and, like any responsible parent, he entered the attorney's office determined to ensure his family would be looked after in the event of his death.

To his wife Ann, William bequeathed their dwelling, just a single room in one of the many terraced houses around the Plymouth docks. As many as six families could be living in each of these tiny three-storey houses, their men at sea for many months. William wanted to be sure that after his death, Ann would have somewhere to live for the rest of her life. To his daughter, Jane[4], William left 20s, and his brother John Cutteford would have William's best woollen doublet. William saved the better portion of his possessions for his only son, who was not yet twenty-one and probably unmarried. To the young George Cutteford, he left the princely sum of £400. Around £10 a year was the usual earnings for a humble sailor of the time, so his sailing exploits had obviously been very profitable for William to have left his son so much.

THE ELIZABETHAN ERA

Elizabeth, the only child of King Henry VIII and his second wife, Anne Boleyn, succeeded her Catholic sister Mary to the throne in 1558, and reigned for forty-four years, until her death in 1603. Elizabeth's court established the Church of England with the monarch as its Supreme Governor, putting an end to the anti-Protestant persecutions of Queen Mary, though this now left Catholics persecuted. When Elizabeth's cousin Mary, Queen of Scots, returned from France, there was a Catholic uprising, determined to put Mary on the English throne.

---

4   PROB 11/285, 'The will of George Cutteford the younger, 13th April 1645.' Held at the National Archives, London. William Cuttiford's will does not give his daughter's name, but George Cutteford the younger bequeaths money to his aunt, Jane Donne, who I presume is his father's sister. (Jane called her son George, making it less likely that she was a sister to Grace Cutteford.)

The uprising failed, and Mary was imprisoned and eventually executed. Her son was subsequently declared James VI of Scotland, inheriting the English throne when Elizabeth I died childless.

Elizabeth's long reign is remembered as one of relative stability and progress in England, an age of global exploration, rising prosperity and the writings of William Shakespeare and John Donne, amongst others. Elizabeth's infamous privateers such as Sir Francis Drake brought home great wealth from their attacks on the Spanish treasure ships returning from South America and the Caribbean. In 1588, Philip II of Spain retaliated by sending the Spanish Armada, a fleet of the largest ships ever built, to invade England's south east coast, but misfortunes and the weather plagued them. The English used 'fire ships' – ships set ablaze and made to drift towards the enemy – to break the Armada's formation. The smaller, faster English ships could then take on the Spanish ships one at a time. The defeat of the Spanish Armada became useful propaganda for Elizabeth and the Protestants; the famous English ships and their charismatic admirals brought both wealth and power to Elizabethan England.

As executor of the will, William Cutteford appointed his best friend, John Maynard, who was also one of the witnesses to the signing of the will. The Maynard family were very influential in Devon, cousins to the Elizabethan hero Sir Francis Drake. Many of the Maynard family were attorneys and philanthropists, establishing almshouses, schools and other charitable establishments in Plymouth and Devon in the sixteenth and seventeenth centuries. John Maynard's descendant namesake became a famous attorney who would influence events in England throughout the seventeenth century.

It was this friendship between William Cutteford and the elder John Maynard that would decide the fate of

Cutteford's descendants. As William sat in the attorney's office, the clerk's pen carefully recording his wishes for the future in a series of intricate pronouncements that William himself could not read, he would have realised that the sea was no future for his son. William would have felt the importance of the man behind the desk. At that moment, William might have dreamed of his son becoming a clerk, perhaps even an attorney, and the philanthropist John Maynard was the man to make that happen.

It was a friendship that would have an astonishing outcome, for just thirty years later, the grandson of William Cutteford would become one of the wealthiest men in Devon. The notorious Mary Howard would be instrumental in his success.

In 1582, however, William Cutteford had only his son's future in mind. John Maynard's relative Alexander was an attorney living in Tavistock and it is quite possible he took on a young apprentice as a clerk, one George Cutteford. Certainly by 1607, George was himself established as an attorney in Tavistock.[5]

George would never have any formal qualifications – there was not the money for him to enter the realms of the Inns of Court in London where lawyers were trained, and George Cutteford was just the son of a sailor, so had no status for such admission. The Inns of Court were there for the sons of landowners and wealthy men, with members of the landed gentry as guarantors for their rent and working space, and the Cutteford family had never owned any land. They were common people; the name Cutteford, in its many different spellings, could be found throughout the south west; possibly related to the first farmers in Chard in Somerset, who were drawn to the south west during the conscriptions of Henry VIII, desperate for fighting men to go to sea to defend his

5   George Cutteford is registered as an attorney in Devon in 1607, in the
    research of the O'Quinn Law Library, University of Houston. See http://aalt.
    law.uh.edu/Attorneys/attpages/FullAttorneyList1607.html.

coastlines against the French.[6] There is still a place called Cuttifords Door in Somerset. 'Cutty' meant something short or small, often referring to a small tobacco pipe or a spoon. 'Ford' was the old word for a river crossing, so at some time the family must have derived the name from a small river crossing near where they lived.

INNS OF COURT

In the seventeenth century there were four Inns of Court in London, established in the fourteenth century for the training of lawyers: Gray's Inn, Lincoln's Inn, the Inner Temple and the Middle Temple. The Temples were established on land formerly owned by the Knights Templar, and subsequently the Hospitallers. There was also a Serjeants Inn for the training of specialist Serjeants at Law, whose work is dramatically portrayed in the series of *Shardlake* books by C.J. Sansom. The Inns of Court were described by Sir Edmund Coke in 1602 as England's third university, along with Oxford and Cambridge, training those heading for a career in the Law as well as educating the sons of nobility and landowners who required good knowledge of contractual law. The education was expensive, and candidates for entry to the courts, as well as being themselves wealthy, had to provide the names of two wealthy landowners as guarantors for their rent and living expenses. This was education for the elite. Most attorneys in England, little more than clerks, were trained through apprenticeships.

Sir Walter Raleigh was a famous member of the Middle Temple – and proved to be a skilled advocate in his own trials. Sir Francis Drake, though not a member, also had close ties with the Middle Temple. The Cup Board, the table where graduating barristers stand to write their names into

---

6   For a well-researched, wonderful description of the wars of King Henry VIII, see C.J. Sansom's novel of the Tudor period, *Heartstone,* 2010.

the Inn's books, is made from the fore hatch of Sir Francis' famous ship *The Golden Hind*.[7]

Men from the southern regions of England would have been conscripted into the Elizabethan navies to guard the south-west English ports in times of war and piracy. Around Exmouth, the Cuttiford name was frequently misspelled as Cutteford, as Cutters were the ships most often used by the customs men, themselves called 'cutters' or cutter men. By the seventeenth century, the homes around Exmouth and nearby Plymouth were filled with families of the sea-going Cuttefords.

So George Cutteford, son of William, found himself educated at one of Maynard's charity schools and possibly apprenticed to a prominent attorney in Tavistock. After the Dissolution of the Monasteries by Henry VIII, the town was still in disarray. Today, it is a quiet though substantial and successful town in the heart of Dartmoor. In the late sixteenth century, Tavistock was a market and a stannary town, struggling at times, housing workers for the local tin mines, the cloisters of the old Abbey now appropriated into tenements and rough housing for the poor and under-paid.[8]

THE STANNARY TOWNS OF DEVON

Devon and Cornwall were major mining regions in the sixteenth and seventeenth century. Certain towns, called Stannaries – 'stannary' derived from the Latin for tin – co-ordinated all mining, smelting, and the assaying and taxation of ingots of tin metal before sale. In Devon, the Stannary towns were Tavistock, Plympton, Ashburton and Chagford, and Stannary Courts were established to administer each tin-working district; to settle any disputes and to put

---

7   See http://www.middletemple.org.uk/the_inn/History_of_the_Inn
8   Woodcock, 2008, Chapter 3, pp. 33-46.

thieves, debtors and fraudsters on trial. Convicted criminals were then locked up in Lydford Castle, which had a terrifying reputation. Over time, the Stannary Courts also gained a fearsome reputation for pronouncing brutal punishments for those stealing tin – one thief, it is said, was made to swallow molten tin, while another was nailed to rocks on the moors and forced to pull the nails out himself or risk dying of exposure. These stories are probably based on myths, circulated widely to deter anyone thinking of stealing valuable ore from the mines.

When there was a need to change the statutes that regulated the tin industry in Devon, a Stannary Parliament or Great Court would be convened, held in the open air at Crockern Tor, located in Dartmoor as a central point between the four stannary towns. The Tor was reputedly named after Old Crockern, an ancient god of the moors, sometimes described as a spectral figure on horseback galloping across the moorland on his skeletal horse, his phantom hounds running alongside.[9]

———————————

Tavistock's most prominent families at that time included the Fitz family who, as well as making money as counsellors-at-law, had married into money from tin-mining and had acquired extensive lands – over 4,000 acres, and more than thirty properties in Devon, Cornwall and around London.[10] In today's money, they were billionaires. They built their family home, the manor house of Fitzford, on an extensive estate; it was erected by the old crossing of the river Tavy that runs through Tavistock. All that remains of the old Fitzford manor is

———————————

9 See Greeves, 1987, for his excellent research into Devon's tin-mining industry – any mistakes I make in the book are most definitely my own. For stories of Old Crockern, see, http://www.legendarydartmoor.co.uk/crockern_tor.html

10 Radford, 1890. The properties in the Fitz estate are also listed in document 2741 M/T/1, the deed poll of Dame Mary Grenville conveying her property to her son George Howard, dated 1661. Held at Devon Record Office.

the gatehouse, though even this was rebuilt in the nineteenth century. There are the Fitzford cottages nearby, built much later, and some small holdings with chickens and such, and Tavistock College now occupies the land that was the grounds to the manor.

The family built two wells at natural springs – which still exist – on Dartmoor called Fice's or Fitz's Wells; the first near Okehampton, the second, which bears the date 1568 and the initials JF, near Princetown.[11] The spring that serviced the Fitzford manor, with water sourced from Dartmoor, was located where Boughthayes Road now meets the Callington Road, as the land rises just north west of Tavistock town centre. Sadly, every trace of the house itself is gone, but it seems that Mary Howard has not left her old home just yet – it is from the Fitzford gatehouse that she rides every night in her spirit coach to Okehampton. For Mary Howard was the daughter of the infamous Sir John Fitz.

To the Fitz family of Fitzford was born a son, John. His father was a respected man in the Tavistock community who, following a successful career as a counsellor-at-law, had retired early and devoted his free time at Fitzford to the study of astrology. As John's mother went into labour, his father cast the baby's horoscope – and was horrified by the result. It seemed that the positions of the planets promised a great terror to come. The father urged the midwife, in vain, to delay the birth by just one hour if humanly possible; the consequences of the timing of the boy's birth looked to be dire. But the baby was born on time, and in time the horoscope's warnings would be realised.

John Fitz was just fourteen when his father died in 1590. His father's tomb can still be found in Tavistock's parish church. Too young to take up his position as heir of the estate, John Fitz was placed in the care of the Court of Wards, and from there came under the guardianship of Sir Arthur Gorges, a poet and

11 Radford, 1890. Dr Tom Greeves also tells me there is a conduit house at Boughthayes which was built by Mary Fitz's grandfather, Sir John Fitz.

translator and an associate of the famous privateer Sir Walter Raleigh. It seems that John's mother, Mary, had been unable to purchase the wardship, so Fitzford was let to strangers and John Fitz's mother moved to the neighbouring estate of Walreddon (which still bears her initials carved into the stone over the entrance, MF, with the date 1591).[12] She eventually re-married, choosing one Sir Christopher Harris, an ally of Sir Francis Drake, and moved to his Radford estate near Plymstock.

THE COURT OF WARDS

In the late sixteenth and early seventeenth centuries, Sir Edmund Coke presided over the Court of Wards, established by King Henry VIII at a time when many wealthy landowners were dying in his wars, leaving under-age heirs at the mercy of corrupt relations. Henry VIII intended that a Court of Wards should care for these wealthy children, with suitable guardians often out-bidding each other for the role and the King pocketing the fee. On coming of age, the wards themselves would then be required to pay a large fee to the King to be released from their wardship.

For the King's coffers, it was a wonderful arrangement, but it was not so beneficial for the children concerned. The system designed to provide better care for these children quickly gave way to corruption and was heavily criticised for separating families, but the Court of Wards remained a fixture of wealthy society for much of the seventeenth century.

In the 1640s, George Cutteford's family friend Sir John Maynard would stand in the House of Commons advocating the abolition of the Court of Wards and Liveries (as it became) and all feudal wardships, but the wardships system was not formally abolished until 27 November 1656. On the Court's demise, all its papers were packed up and stored

---

12 Radford, 1890.

in a fish yard by Westminster Hall, an ancient building within the current precinct of the Houses of Parliament. In the seventeenth century, shops and stalls were located in and around Westminster Hall, offering supplies to the lawyers and politicians. Sadly the bizarre location for the storage of the Court's papers has left many of the historic documents in a very poor state, frequently unreadable. They were rescued in the early 1700s, but didn't enter the Public Record Office until the mid-1800s.[13]

John Fitz appears to have had a pleasant upbringing, despite the circumstances. At twenty, he was described as a handsome fellow, though there were early signs of boisterous behaviour and a quick temper; quite the romantic hero, though still too young to come into his fortune. By 1596, John Fitz had married Bridget Courtenay and their first and only child, Mary, was born. John was then twenty; Bridget was about twenty-three, which was an unusual alliance at the time.[14]

 Bridget was the second daughter of Sir William Courtenay of Powderham Castle in Exmouth, so it is surprising that she

-----

13 From the Public Record Office, on the website for the record summary of the Court of Wards and Liveries: 'The terrible condition of many of the records of the Court of Wards and Liveries is explained by the fact that after the court's demise they were kept in a fish yard near Westminster Hall. They were removed in the early eighteenth century to rooms next to the House of Lords belonging to Black Rod and from there to the Chapter House in 1732. They came from there to the Public Record Office in 1859-1860.' See http://www.nationalarchives.gov.uk/catalogue/DisplayCatalogueDetails.asp?CATID=258&CATLN=1&FullDetails=True

14 There are discrepancies in the records available concerning the birth-date for Bridget Courtenay. Tudor place at www.tudorplace.com.ar gives her year of birth as around 1572, and her brother Francis and William were born 1576 and 1580 respectively. (See http://www.tudorplace.com.ar/COURTENAY2.htm#Bridget COURTENAY1) Other records state her year of birth as 1580, so she may have been fifteen or sixteen at the time of her marriage to John Fitz. Whatever her age, her father Sir William Courtenay was determined to ensure her safety, and the future ownership of the Fitz estates, by all possible means.

had not been married off at a younger age to other wealthy or more influential suitors. John Fitz was still under twenty-one, and so had not yet come into his inheritance. The arrangement therefore suggests hurried necessity – with the spinster Bridget, perhaps, falling for the young man's charms, and becoming pregnant. It also suggests that the marriage was arranged deliberately before John Fitz was twenty-one. John's guardian, probably with the help of Sir Walter Raleigh, could easily have been coerced into helping the Courtenays obtain a claim to the vast Fitz estates.

Whatever reasons for the marriage, when his daughter moved into Fitzford manor, Sir William made certain she would be cared for, and placed one of his associates nearby, residing with John Fitz's mother at Walreddon to keep a close eye on the 'happy couple'. There are certainly signs that Sir William did not trust his new son-in-law, and he was right to be wary. From the day of her birth to all the way through to her modern legend, Mary's name would be associated with calamity and death.

Mary's name would also be affiliated with money. Her father was a rich man, and her mother, Bridget, was from a powerful family; Mary's grandfather was Deputy Lord Warden of the Stannaries. Queen Elizabeth appointed Sir Walter Raleigh as Lord Warden from 1585 to 1603, with his friend Sir William Courtenay as his Deputy.[15] This essentially put them in charge of the Royal Mint. Those controlling the Stannaries, like Raleigh and Courtenay, were very powerful men indeed.

As a Stannary Town, Tavistock attracted wealthy men like John Fitz, and attorneys like George Cutteford, who seems to have arrived in Tavistock at about the time of the birth of John Fitz's daughter. Anyone casting a horoscope for Mary at her birth would not have been pleased with its ominous portents.

Sir William Courtenay, however, would have been delighted at Mary's birth. Though not a son, she would still inherit all

---

15 The Federation of Old Cornwall Societies gives an excellent account of the history of tax collection, stannary towns and the role of the Lord of the Stannaries. See http://smugglers.oldcornwall.org/index.html

the Fitz properties and fortune, an impressive list which included Fitzford, Walreddon and its estates; Rushey Green manor, with extensive grounds in Lewisham (then located in the county of Kent, though now part of London); and, most importantly, Okehampton Park and its castle, which had not been in the Courtenay family for some time. Mary also inherited Woolsgrove and Meldon manors, properties at Milemead, Paswell, Bolthouse, Roundwood, Langham Wood, Burchwood, Crelake, Dowermeadow, Whitchurch, Bere Ferris, Crediton, Spreyton, Inwardleigh, Brentor, Lamerton, Milton Abbot, Kilworthy, Sampford Spiney, Walkhampton, Hayes End at Tamerton Foliot (now part of Plymouth), Withecombe, Boyton, and Calstock, Hornacott in Cornwall, and St Saviour in Southwark, on the south bank of the Thames nearly opposite the Tower (then part of Surrey, but now part of London). In short, she had 4,000 acres in four counties, with an income exceeding £1,000 a year.

THE COURTENAYS OF OKEHAMPTON CASTLE[16]

Within months of the arrival of William the Conqueror in 1066, William sent his cousins and brothers-in-law to build a chain of mound forts along the spine of England's south west peninsula, including Okehampton Castle. With Viking tenacity and versed in Latin scriptures, these Normans – the name a variant on Norsemen – took absolute control of the region, precious for its production of tin, copper and wool.

The Norman Sheriff, Baldwin de Brionne, had married into William's family, and in around 1068 established Okehampton, on the banks of the river Okement, as the

---

16 Reproduced from my article on Okehampton Castle in Dartmoor Online magazine (www.dartmooronline.co.uk), with kind permission of the editors, Elisabeth Stanbrook and Dr Tom Greeves, MA, PhD. Also see Mildren, 1987 and Radford, 2002.

administrative centre of his Devon lands. For the castle, he chose a shale spur on a wooded hillside, and built a mound to support a Norman fort. Brionne's heirs – a long line of women – would continue to run the family estates, including Hawisia de Ancourt who married Reginald Courtenay in 1173. At that time, the castle was not much more than a simple motte, a functional stone fort, but Reginald Courtenay had grander plans for his new estate.

In France, Reginald Courtenay was born into a prominent family, but he himself had no land. He accompanied Eleanor of Aquitaine to Britain where she became Queen of England by her marriage to the Norman King Henry II. Reginald was granted lands in what is now Sutton Courtenay, and established a small manor there, but marriage to Hawisia brought greater fortunes in Devon, and he chose Okehampton Castle to be his stately home. Of course, a simple motte was not nearly impressive enough for a man of his new stature, and he set about building a luxurious castle, with high towers, and many bedrooms, and a vast dining hall for entertaining his many friends. For their entertainment, he developed the forests around into a deer park, still known as Okehampton Park. Reginald was renowned for his sumptuous banquets and hunting parties. There would soon be no land-owner in Devon to rival the Courtenays, and they held Okehampton for 350 years.

Religious divisions would eventually destroy their fortunes. In the 1500s, Reginald's descendant Henry Courtenay was in a very powerful position. Now Earl of Devon and Marquess of Exeter, he was a cousin and boyhood friend to King Henry VIII, and had a legitimate claim to the throne. From Okehampton, he administered the west of England and was due to claim vast lands with Henry VIII's plans for the Dissolution of the Monasteries.

Anne Boleyn, Henry VIII's second wife, was jealous of the Courtenays' influence on the monarchy, and set about destroying them. The Courtenays were Catholics, and had maintained an alliance with Henry VIII's first wife, Katherine of Aragon, a Spanish Catholic, now humiliated by the divorce. The Courtenays remained steadfast in their loyalty to the King, but rumours reached King Henry that disgruntled Catholics in the south west were plotting to put Henry Courtenay on the throne. There was probably some truth in this; the divorce and subsequent split with the Catholic Church were very unpopular.

King Henry's reaction was brutal. He had Henry Courtenay, his wife, their young son, Edward, and their Catholic allies arrested, imprisoned and brought to trial for treason. The King destroyed Okehampton Castle, with orders for it never to be rebuilt, as a warning to all who might threaten the throne.

The Courtenays' son and heir Edward, just twelve years old, would remain in prison for the next sixteen years, watching first his father dragged from the cell and beheaded in 1538, and then witnessing his mother and her friends going insane in the horrific prison conditions. Edward's mother was released in time but she was forced to leave her son behind, now alone in a decrepit cell.

Eventually Edward was released, much to the delight of the daughter of Katherine of Aragon, now Queen Mary. Mary took a fancy to the handsome Edward. Both Catholics, there was talk of marriage, but (as in most relationships) there was a misunderstanding – Edward thought Mary was no longer interested, with rumours of her marriage to King Philip of Spain, and Edward tried instead to woo the favour of her younger sister, Elizabeth. This was not a good move. Mary, in jealous fury, had Edward imprisoned again, then exiled to Europe, where – in Padua, they say – he was poisoned in 1566. It was a sad end to the Courtenay line.

Another branch of the Courtenay family would eventually lay claim to the ruins of Okehampton Castle and its park, when in 1596 Bridget Courtenay married Sir John

Fitz, but it would be many years before the Courtenays could call Okehampton Park their own.

———————

Sir William Courtenay had recently found himself in some financial embarrassment. In the late 1500s, he had been awarded Powderham Castle by Queen Elizabeth for his services in Ireland. He had commanded a force of 3,000 men in Devon and the defences of Dorset, and continued to advise the Crown on appropriate measures to defend the coast against pirates. On marrying the widow of Sir Francis Drake, he also inherited her estates, including Buckland Abbey. However, his fortunes suffered considerably when his plantations in Ireland were destroyed by the Irish Rebellion. The prospect of acquiring the lands and wealth of the Fitz family therefore was certainly attractive, but the behaviour of his son-in-law would soon prove to be a danger to his family's future.

THE MUNSTER PLANTATIONS

Under Queen Elizabeth I, Sir William Courtenay had become one of the 'undertakers' or primary investors for the English Munster plantations, involving the forced appropriation of Irish lands by English Lords. Sir William was contracted to 'undertake' the planting of vast acres of Irish lands, introducing English settlers and Protestant tenants, establishing new towns, and fortifying the settlements and farms against attack; 500,000 acres of Irish land were confiscated and planted by English farmers, but the English population never rose much above 5,000 and the settlements were scattered and difficult to defend. The Irish, not unsurprisingly, rebelled against English rule. When the Irish rebels reached Munster, the outnumbered English settlers ran away without much opposition. Sir William and his sons took up the fight, and his son George remained settled in Ireland to defend their lands. The rebellion was eventually put down by brutal force in 1601-1603 and the plantations re-established, but the finances of the original undertakers like Sir William Courtenay suffered terribly. Instead of owning extensive lands in Ireland with thousands of tenants, Sir William found himself at the mercy of the money-lenders. Sir William's eldest son and heir died in 1603 after returning from the battles in Ireland, leaving his second eldest son, Frances, eventually to inherit the struggling Powderham estates.

John Fitz's marriage to Bridget became fractious from the day of Mary's birth. Her parents argued constantly and John Fitz, in a furious temper, eventually threw baby Mary and her mother out of Fitzford. Mother and child fled in terror to the place of Mary's birth, the neighbouring estate of Walreddon, which was occupied at that time by Sir William Courtenay's associate Richard Halse.[17] It is very likely that George Cutteford was also living at Walreddon at the time.

To organise the customs officers and the operations of the local court, Sir William appointed an Under-Sheriff, a man called Halse whose family's own success had brought them Kenedon Manor near Powderham. This Mr Halse was not a man to be crossed. He had even successfully prosecuted one of the younger Courtenays for theft and other misdemeanours.[18]

At Sir William's request, Mr Halse sent his eldest son Richard to secure Bridget Courtenay's interests in Tavistock and the Fitz estate.

---

17 The Tavistock records show Richard Halse was very busy with land deals around Tavistock in the early seventeenth century, and document D1508M/Moger/388, held at Devon Record Office, is a conveyance of Walreddon Manor from Richard Halse and his wife Anna to Sir Francis Glanville and Edward Skitrett in 1623. Interesting to note that Mr Skitrett – or possibly Skirrett – was very likely related to the Cuttefords by marriage.

18 See James Courtenay's confession to a shocking number of robberies and misdemeanours in 1538, with the thieves bought before Mr Halse, Under-Sheriff of Devon, at British History Online www.british-history.ac.uk, specific URL http://193.39.212.226/report.aspx?compid=75786

Young Richard Halse had just completed his studies at the Inner Temple, one of the Inns of Court in London, and was now qualified as an attorney.[19] Sometime around 1598, Richard moved into Walreddon Manor, taking with him his wife Ann and their two sons.[20] But John Fitz proved to be a very violent man, and Richard Halse soon realised he needed some help.

Meanwhile, in 1599, a Devon attorney called John Pearse had issues with Richard Halse's cousin, Nicholas.[21] Nicholas Halse was the collector of customs and subsidies for the ports of Plymouth and Fowey, and had recently given his daughter Grace a house in Plympton as part of her marriage settlement to one of his customs officers, George Cutteford.[22]

The attorney John Pearse claimed that the arrangement with George Cutteford left one of his clients out of pocket, and the matter was disputed over many years. The sums involved were relatively small – £20 here, another £40 there – but they were substantial enough for John Pearse to refer his complaint against George Cutteford and his father-in-law to the Court of the Star Chamber in London.

For George Cutteford to be prosecuted in the Star Chamber was a serious matter indeed, and John Pearse is damning in his descriptions of the defendants' misdealings, frequently referring to 'corruption', 'guile' and 'fraud'. These are words not used lightly in appeals to the Star Chamber.[23]

---

19 Richard Halse entered the Inner Temple on 14 February 1597. See their archive database: http://www.innertemple.org.uk/archive/itad/index.asp

20 Document 107/85c from 1615, held at Plymouth and West Devon Record Office, mentions Jerome and John, sons of Richard Halse.

21 STAC 8/230/27, Pearse vs Hals and Cutteford, 1614, held at the National Archives in London. There are a number of ways Halse is spelled in the records, including Hals and sometimes Hales. I have standardised it as Halse. Also, John Pearse is listed as an attorney in Devon, in the research of the O'Quinn Law Library, University of Houston. See http://aalt.law.uh.edu/Attorneys/attpages/FullAttorneyList1607.html,

22 STAC 8/230/27, Pearse vs Hals and Cutteford, 1614, held at the National Archives in London.

23 STAC 8/230/27, Pearse vs Hals and Cutteford, 1614, held at the National Archives in London.

THE STAR CHAMBER

The Star Chamber was named after the pattern of stars on the ceiling in the room where the court officials met in Westminster to hear appeals, petitions and matters of redress. The court had evolved from the courts of earlier monarchs, and the officials in the seventeenth century could pronounce any sentence except the death sentence. Punishments could be barbaric and seem medieval, frequently involving maiming the poor defendants in public, such as cutting off ears or noses, making the Star Chamber synonymous with cruelty and thereby very unpopular with the people. As ordinary courts of law evolved and became more systematic, the Star Chamber remained a powerful though anachronistic court of law, practically and legally distinct from any Parliament. By 1640, the Star Chamber would become notorious for imprisoning and torturing political prisoners without public trial or the need for witness testimony.

However, George Cutteford's friendship with John Maynard seems to have rescued him. The Star Chamber referred the matter back to the local magistrate Elize Hele, an influential man who would become Treasurer to King James I, and who was himself a renowned philanthropist and close associate of John Maynard. The covering note to Elize Hele refers to 'George Cutteford, your cousin'[24], suggesting there was at least a distant relationship, probably between the Halse and the Hele families. Elize Hele arranged for an out-of-court settlement that admitted no guilt on behalf of the defendants but still ended the matter to everyone's satisfaction.

---

24 STAC 8/230/27, Pearse vs Hals and Cutteford, 1614, held at the National Archives in London. I have discovered that the Heles and the Halses were related by marriage, so 'cousin' is an accurate description of George Cutteford's relationship to Elize Hele.

This was not the first time George's father-in-law had been in trouble. In 1595, Nicholas Halse was called to answer a complaint by a Mr Watts, an alderman of London.[25] It seems that Nicholas Halse, the customs official, had obtained by guile some very precious 'cochinella and indico' from Mr Watts' ship, the *Jewel*, and Nicholas was forced to make reparations to Mr Watts. Perhaps it was Nicholas Halse who got his son-in-law into trouble with the Star Chamber in the first place, for George Cutteford would soon be disassociating himself from his father-in-law's corrupt activities.

THE CUTTERS OF THE SEVENTEENTH CENTURY

In the seventeenth century, life as a customs officer in south-west England was hard, constantly patrolling the coasts on the look-out for smugglers bringing in contraband or attempting to steal tin and other valuable commodities being transported.[26] The first customs officers in England were appointed in 1294, and they acquired the nickname 'cutters' or 'cutter men' because the ships they used were Cutters; single-masted sloops, small but quick and easy to manoeuvre. They were regularly attacked by pirates in much larger sea-going vessels, so the Cutters were usually out-manned and out-gunned, and frequently had to withdraw.

It was a thankless task. Slave traders frequented the coastline, stealing people away to be sold in North Africa or the East, or to work the ships. Corsairs were another significant threat – privateers employed by the French government to raid foreign ships, including the English. If captured they would claim the rights of prisoners-of-war rather than be tried as criminals.

---

25 See details of the case at British History Online, at http://www.british-history.ac.uk/report.aspx?compid=111643, 17 May, 1595.

26 Again, the Federation of Old Cornwall Societies gives an excellent account of the history of tax collection, smuggling, slavery, cutter men, and the stannaries. See http://smugglers.oldcornwall.org/index.html

Customs officers were engaged in a constant war against these many raiders, fighting to secure the harbours from attack, retrieving captured slaves and searching ships for contraband, often out-manoeuvred by the French and the North African pirates, the latter frequently referred to as Turkish corsairs. To be a customs officer or 'cutter' you had to be quick-thinking and cunning, and always ready to fight.

The cutter men, however, had a bad reputation. They weren't popular, certainly not with those locals who were benefiting from the pirates and smugglers, and they were also thought to be corrupt. Customs officials and those who employed them could make substantial amounts of money by pocketing bribes, taking percentages, and making some of the cargoes 'disappear'. Customs and later excise, the inland taxes introduced in 1643, were seen by some as lucrative trades, despite the many dangers.

The coastlines of south west England, now popular with tourists for their pleasant beaches and peaceful surrounds, were in the seventeenth century hazardous and lawless places. From a modern perspective, customs officers and those then responsible for policing the harbours might be seen as sometimes using the law to their own advantage, but they were tough people working in a dangerous and volatile environment, defending an extensive coastline, and struggling to protect their own families, as well as the interests of the Crown.

From an early age, it seems, George Cutteford had influential friends. The Maynards certainly remained family friends. George's marriage into the Halse family improved his social and economic status, but his father-in-law's reputation was a disadvantage to a man with ambitions.

Historians have so far regarded George Cutteford as just an attorney caught up in the fight over the Fitz estates, innocently unaware or uninvolved in the financial misdealings that would eventually destroy his life. His experiences with John Pearse and his early work as a customs officer in dangerous circumstances, however, reveal a man who may have been struggling to stay honest. Living in a corrupt age, he learned to use his powerful friends and in-laws to his family's advantage. The Pearse case shows that George Cutteford did not simply find himself an apprenticeship in Tavistock, but in fact started his career as a customs officer in Plymouth and married into the influential Halse family.

At an early age, George Cutteford seems to have shown considerable financial dexterity, which would have appealed to Sir William Courtenay (and his agent, Richard Halse) in their battles over Fitzford. When Richard Halse moved to Tavistock to secure Bridget Courtenay's claim to the Fitz fortunes, sometime in 1596, his cousin, George Cutteford, was exactly the kind of man Halse needed to handle the violent John Fitz. George would have been pleased to have the opportunity to distance himself from his corrupt father-in-law.

Such success would have delighted George's father, William, who could never have imagined his son rising to such status in society, simply through an initial friendship with John Maynard. George's financial acumen would have been a credit to the family, delighted that their son had found himself a profession more secure than life at sea.

The journey to Tavistock, however, would prove to be a difficult and dangerous expedition.

Many historians believe that George Cutteford was just a local Tavistock attorney employed by Mary when she was about sixteen, but in fact it seems that George Cutteford was a customs officer who moved to Walreddon with his in-laws, the Halse family, at around the time of Mary's birth. He was almost certainly there as an agent for Sir William Courtenay to secure the safety of Mary's fortune by any means necessary.

It was a role that would cost George Cutteford his life.

Chapter Two

The Terror Begins

In June 1599, with John Fitz's wife and child safely out of his way at nearby Walreddon, he invited some friends to his Fitzford manor to dine. The dinner lasted all night and descended into drunken revelry that lasted until noon the following day. The inebriated John Fitz boasted to the party that he was no tenant farmer. Every foot of land in all his estates, he declared, he owned in freehold. It belonged to his family forever. Nicholas Slanning, from nearby Bickleigh, tried to correct his host, saying that John actually owed him rent for a parcel of land which rightfully belonged to Slanning.[1]

John Fitz rose to his feet and drew his dagger in fury at being corrected. Slanning countered the attack with a dagger of his own – it may seem strange that these men kept their daggers close by them at parties, but of course knives were not standard tableware in Elizabethan times and guests would frequently use their own daggers to cut their meat. Still, attacking each other with dining implements over the table does seem ludicrous even for the late sixteenth century.

Slanning successfully defended himself, and their mutual friends managed to calm the situation, allowing Slanning and his servant to ride back towards Bickleigh.

On coming to a steep and rough descent, perhaps the Walkham river valley, Slanning let his servant walk the horses

---

1 Radford, 1890, and very well retold in Dacre, 2010.

The grave of Elizabeth I.

while he strolled home.[2] Without warning, they were suddenly accosted by Fitz and his drunken cohorts, armed
and on horseback, hell-bent on continuing the argument.
Fitz demanded that Slanning's insult be avenged and ordered
his men to draw their swords and descend upon the poor
man. Following a brief skirmish, Fitz and his men sheathed
their swords and all seemed over – until one of Fitz's men
teased his friend with 'What, child's play? Come to fight and
now put up your sword?' Slanning was still wearing his long
spurs and, stepping back, his foot caught in the ground. Sadly,
at this same moment John Fitz, annoyed by his friend's com-
ment, chose to thrust his sword, and Slanning was brutally – if
accidentally – killed.

Nicholas Slanning's death was just the first of many, often
in mysterious circumstances, that would haunt the Fitz estates.

John Fitz rightly feared prosecution. The outcry against
the killing of a good man like Nicholas Slanning was heard
across the county, with Slanning's memorial at Bickleigh
well attended by concerned friends and devastated relatives.
Fitz managed to escape to France until the Courtenay family,
later that same year, secured a pardon from the Queen for the
delinquent. John's pardon would cost him the Fitz estate, which
was entailed away from him to his wife Bridget – and thereaf-
ter, in a clever manipulation of events, to the Courtenay family.

Unfortunately, the murder did nothing to change John Fitz's
ways. He returned as wilful, drunken and haughty as ever, much
to the disappointment of the townsfolk and the Courtenays.

In 1603, James I came to the throne in some controversy. His
mother, Mary Queen of Scots, had, after all, been executed by
the previous monarch. By way of appeasement, James knighted

---

2   Radford, 1890, p. 71. Mrs Radford suggests a slight variation to the story here.
    In Tavistock there used to be 'old hollow ways', frequently used for riding in
    the sixteenth and seventeenth century. Apparently these old paths became
    uncomfortably hot in summer. Riding home in June 1599, Nicholas Slanning
    dismounted and left his servant to take the horses down these old hollow
    ways, while Nicholas strolled across the cooler meadows.

all his allies and anyone of influence – about 400 members of the landed gentry were bribed with titles, including John Fitz.

Once back at Fitzford, though, Sir John refused to behave like a true knight, and joined 'the wrong crowd'; his new-found friends included one notorious local criminal called Lusty Jack. John and his drunken associates wreaked havoc on the town. They broke windows, dragged men out of their beds, quarrelled in public houses and out into the street, and fought battles between themselves. One of the town's constables was almost killed in the many skirmishes. John's behaviour grew so scandalous that even his friends began to shun him. Fitzford manor fell into a state of disrepair – and Sir William Courtenay was furious.

KING JAMES I

In 1567, at just three months old, James was crowned James VI, King of Scots, after his mother Mary Queen of Scots was forced to abdicate; she was, of course, later executed by her cousin, Queen Elizabeth I. In 1603, he inherited the English throne, Elizabeth having died without issue. He was crowned James I of England and Scotland. A talented scholar, he had a dark interest in witchcraft, considering practitioners deserving of the death penalty.[3]

As a believer in the Divine Right of Kings, James considered his crown to have been given to him by God, and felt he was answerable only to God rather than Parliament. During his reign, he called Parliament only when he

---

3   In 1597, influenced by his personal involvement in the North Berwick witch trials, the man who would be crowned King James I published his book *Daemonologie*, in support of witch hunting, advocating the most severe punishment for these 'slaves of the Devil'.

needed money to support his extravagant lifestyle.[4]
He was renowned for his many male liaisons, forming a
particular regard for George Villiers, the handsome Duke
of Buckingham. Whether they were actually lovers is still
debated, though James was already old at forty-seven and
becoming feeble when he first met Villiers. James' descriptions of the handsome, dashing Villiers suggest that Villiers
reminded James of his eldest son, Henry, who had tragically
died young, leaving James' sickly second son Charles as heir
to the throne. George Villiers replaced the preferred son in
James' affections, giving Villiers a very strong influence over
James's court.

In 1605, when the Gunpowder Plot – an attempt by
Catholic sympathisers to blow up the Protestant King
James and Parliament – failed, James I sanctioned harsh
measures against non-conformists. When James died, he
left the country in severe financial difficulties and heading
into war with Spain, yet James's twenty-two year reign was
considered by his contemporaries as one of relative peace.
Perhaps, as Charles's reign headed for the disasters of the
English Civil War, they looked back on his father's time
with some nostalgia.

In 1605, the children of Nicholas Slanning reached adulthood
and decided to sue John Fitz for compensation for causing
their father's death. Fitz was summoned to appear in court in
London to answer the charges. While travelling to London with
a servant, John's guilt weighted heavily upon him, but more so
his concern at the retribution Sir William Courtenay would
exact upon him if he lost substantial amounts of the estate in

---

4   It seems King James I convened Parliament only four times during his reign.
    The 1605 session was marred by the Gunpowder Plot. In 1604, 1610 and the
    so-called 'Addled' Parliament of 1614, James argued with Parliament over
    money, the last Parliament dismissed after just eight weeks. James then ruled
    without Parliament until 1621.

the court case. He firmly believed that Sir William Courtenay's agents were after him and would kill him on the road before he could reach the court; his fears were wholly justified.

After a long journey, John and his servant arrived at Kingston-on-Thames and spent the night. John Fitz was so deranged by this time that he could not sleep, and, hearing noises, he rose from his bed, summoned his horse and rode off, refusing the company of his servant who he believed might be there to kill him. He was never to return.

At midnight, he drew up at the Anchor, a small tavern in Twickenham, and hammered at the door, raising the publican, Daniel Alley, and the poor man's wife out of bed. Fitz demanded shelter for the rest of the night, but Daniel's tavern was small, not really a suitable place for a man like Sir John Fitz to stay – and anyway, as Daniel protested, there were no beds left. John's response was so loud and abusive that, worried there would be complaints from the neighbours, Daniel let the man in, and gave John his own bed, which meant Daniel's wife sleeping with the children.

John was an unruly guest, and his shouting and tossing in the bed kept the whole household awake. At dawn, Daniel decided he may as well leave the tavern early to help a neighbour mowing a meadow, though his wife begged him not to leave her alone with the strange man. The neighbour arrived at the door and spoke with Daniel, and their voices reached Sir John who, in his disordered sleep, thought his enemies had arrived at the tavern to kill him. John Fitz rushed out in his nightgown, drew his sword and killed Daniel Alley. When Daniel's wife screamed in horror, John turned and stabbed her too.

As the sun rose, John was faced with the horror of his actions. In a fit of despair, he stabbed himself. The neighbour was joined by others who had heard the noise, and together they carried the badly wounded John Fitz back into the bed he had just vacated to kill its owner. A surgeon was called for, and his wounds bound up, but John feverishly tore away the bandage and bled to death.

Despite the terrible tragedy for Daniel Alley and his family, there were many who rejoiced at John Fitz's bloody end – not least Sir William Courtenay, whose grand-daughter Mary, just nine years old, now inherited the estate. However, Sir William's plans had not counted on the vagaries of the Court of Wards.

Near Twickenham, the 9th Earl of Northumberland, Sir Henry Percy, was one of the first to hear of John Fitz's death[5] and quickly realised the implications for the Fitz estate. The Earl put in a substantial offer for the guardianship of Mary, declaring it was out of concern for his good friend, her father. Of course, the wealth of the Fitz estates would also have been a significant incentive.

Sir William Courtenay may have put forward a competing bid, but his own finances were in a state of disarray following the collapse of the Munster plantations. Sir William Courtenay accumulated a substantial empire during his lifetime, but still the Courtenays' were struggling with creditors. The Courtenay household was unable to raise sufficient monies to counter the Earl of Northumberland's bid.

And so Mary Fitz was purchased from her family, at just nine years old. Mary was at that time staying with her mother, Bridget, and her grandmother at the Radford estates near Plympton.[6] In 1605, soon after her father's death, Mary was torn from the arms of her mother and grandmother. She would never see either of them again. Through the Court of Wards, Mary was placed under the guardianship of the Earl and taken to live with him at Syon House. It would be many

---

5   Radford, 1890. It is said, on hearing that Sir John Fitz was wounded, the Earl of Northumberland sent his chaplain to assist the wounded man. The Chaplain subsequently, it is believed, published the *Bloodie Book of John Fitz* anonymously in 1605.

6   Radford, 1890.

years before George Cutteford would see Mary again, and
when she returned at last to Fitzford she was a very damaged
and misused young woman.

THE WIZARD EARL

Sir Henry Percy was an unusual character. Renowned for
his interests in the sciences and rumoured to practise the
occult, he was often referred to as the 'Wizard Earl'. Much
of his research was done at Syon House in Richmond,
next to what is now Kew Botanical Gardens, just north of
Twickenham. In the British Museum, in the centre of the
museum's top gallery, stands Sir Percy's armillary sphere, a
model of the universe according to the ancient astrono-
mer Claudius Ptolemy, with the Earth at the centre, and
the sun positioned amidst the heavenly spheres rotating
around the Earth. Probably made in Italy, it has Sir Percy's
coat of arms engraved on the base, supported by three cast-
iron lions. The sphere would have been very expensive
even in the seventeenth century. Sir Percy's fascination with
Renaissance science often led him to forget his duties as
a landowner, and he frequently quarrelled with his tenants
in his demands for money to support his research. During
the reign of Elizabeth I, his family had prospered, but as
a Catholic sympathiser, he was now distrusted by the new
King James I and in 1605, his fortunes were suffering.

His fortunes declined still further when the Earl's
close relation, Thomas Percy, was caught and killed as
one of the plotters who had famously attempted to blow
up the Houses of Parliament. The night before the failed
Gunpowder Plot was discovered, on 4 November 1605, the
plotter Thomas had spent the evening at Syon House, with
the Earl of Northumberland and probably his ward Mary.
Association brought condemnation and the Earl was sub-

sequently tried, found guilty of treasonable behaviour and sent to the Tower.

Sir William Courtenay had personal experience of the Court of Wards. When he was just four years old, his own father had died at the Battle of St Quinton in northern France, and Sir William had been taken into the care of his great grandfather William Paulet, who received some of the Courtenay lands and the wardship as a gift for his service to the Crown whilst fighting in France. Sir William's own father had been a ward of Thomas Cromwell in 1535, so the Courtenays were accustomed to the process. But Mary's wardship and the subsequent loss of the vast Fitz estates would have devastated their financial situation.

Mary's stay at Syon house with the Earl of Northumberland would not last long however. Just a few months later, the Earl was implicated in the Gunpowder Plot against James I and, prosecuted by Sir Edmund Coke, ended up imprisoned for many years in the Tower of London.

By coincidence, Sir Edmund Coke also presided over the Court of Wards, and Mary soon found herself taken to the London home of Lady Hatton, the wife of Sir Edmund Coke, while her guardian languished in the Tower.

THE LEGEND OF LADY HATTON

Lady Elizabeth Hatton, a society beauty, had married Sir Edmund Coke in 1597. She kept her own house, Hatton House in London, having inherited a great wealth from her former husband who had been the heir to Sir Christopher Hatton, Lord Chancellor to Queen Elizabeth I.

Lady Hatton's marriage to Edmund Coke was difficult from the start – first, she retained her former husband's name, much to the embarrassment of her new husband, and second, she was a formidable personality with strong views, which made her, in seventeenth-century terms, a troublesome wife.[7]

Lady Hatton's name is linked to the legend of the Bleeding Heart Yard.[8] The body of one Elizabeth Hatton – wrongly thought to be that of Lady Hatton of Hatton House – was found on the morning of 27 January 1626 in the courtyard that would become known as the Bleeding Heart Yard. Lady Hatton, it is said, had spent the evening of 26 January in the company of the Bishop of Ely, at a ball in Hatton House. Late in the evening, the Spanish Ambassador, Senor Gondomar, arrived, had just one dance with the beautiful Lady Hatton – and then they both disappeared into the night. The following morning, her body was discovered in the courtyard behind the stables of Hatton House. When they found her, she had been torn limb from limb, with her heart still pumping blood onto the cobblestones.

In truth, however, Lady Hatton died quietly in her seventies, in 1646. The urban legend of the Bleeding Heart Yard is a wonderful illustration of how names from the seventeenth century get confused; there were, after all, many women called Elizabeth Hatton – Elizabeth being a very popular name at the time. Over the years, the legend became linked to the wife of Sir Edmund Coke simply because she was a forthright, 'troublesome' wife, not the passive spouse so idealised at the time. Sir Edmund's involvement in the Court of Wards – and the court's appalling treatment of the young Mary Fitz – would have a marked effect on the real Lady Hatton, and the future of her own daughter, Frances Coke.

———————

Though still in the Tower, the 9th Earl of Northumberland arranged a marriage between Mary and his younger brother

7   Fraser, 1984, including p.292, which describes the terms of Lady Hatton's
    separation from Sir Edmund Coke.

8   See one fine example of the telling of the story at: http://www.shadyoldlady.
    com/location.php?loc=756

Sir Alan Percy. On their wedding day, Mary was just twelve; Sir Alan was thirty-two. The disparate ages of the bride and groom caused quite a scandal, even in the seventeenth century. Twelve was the age of consent for women, but any mention of the girl being 'unripe' would delay the nuptials, so Mary was required to stay with Lady Hatton in London for the first few years of her marriage.

Lady Hatton's strong personality had a significant effect on Mary's own response to her situation, as time would tell. Mary would never be one to allow herself to be beaten into submission. Mary soon learned to be submissive when it suited her, manipulative when she wanted to be, and to turn a violent situation to her own advantage.

WOMEN AND MARRIAGE IN THE SEVENTEENTH CENTURY

Women of the lower classes in seventeenth-century England were expected to marry young, but most worked until they were in their twenties before choosing to marry and have children. Although their lives were hard, it is strange to think that the same freedom was not permitted for women of the upper classes. Where money and land was at stake, and there was an urgent need for a male heir, young women in the upper classes were frequently married before they were fourteen and expected to start having children as soon as physically possible.[9]

Fourteen was the legal age for young girls to come into their inheritance – from this age, they officially had a say over who they would marry, in principle if not in fact, so it was in the guardian's best interest to get the marriage arranged before their female ward turned fourteen. (Boys did not come into their inheritance until they were twenty-

---

9   Fraser, 1984, pp. 11 and 12.

one, so their guardians had a little longer to formulate their marriage arrangements.)

Twelve years after Mary moved into Hatton House, King James I would preside over a spectacular wedding ceremony and give away Lady Hatton's daughter, Frances Coke, as a fourteen-year-old bride. Sir Edmund Coke saw the arranged marriage as a means of getting into favour with the flamboyant King. The young bride was beautiful and a very wealthy heiress. The husband was the maniacally insane Sir John Villiers, twenty-six, the younger brother of the King's favourite courtier, the Duke of Buckingham. Sir Edmund Coke needed the King's favour; the Villiers family needed the money. Lady Hatton was horrified.

Lady Hatton attempted to steal away the bride-to-be and find her a more suitable match, but Sir Edmund battered down the door, and after a physical battle over the girl, dragged poor Frances away screaming. Lady Hatton then armed herself with men and pistols, but this second attempt failed and Lady Hatton was charged with attempted kidnapping. The Courts tried to settle the matter by allowing Sir John Villiers to woo the child Frances, but she would not be wooed. Mother and daughter shared their hatred of Sir John – and with good reason. Sir Edmund had Lady Hatton placed under house arrest, and his daughter Frances tied to the bedposts and whipped, more than once, until she consented to the match.

So King James gave away the battered bride, the King happily drinking everyone's health and the next morning visiting the 'happy couple' eager for details of the wedding night. (James was renowned for his vulgar interest in the intimacies of wedding nights, frequently visiting young couples in their wedding beds.)

Lady Hatton was at first refused permission to attend the wedding; then her husband changed his mind, and she was ordered to attend – at which point she declined, declaring she was sick. She was probably haunted by memories of what had happened to her ward Mary Fitz just nine years earlier, and horrified that the same had happened to her own daughter.

Mary, at twelve, was an unusually young bride. The arrangement was seen as distasteful, but the motives of the groom were clear. Sir Alan was in some financial embarrassment – he was struggling to repay a loan to his brother – and easy access to the Fitz estates was an ideal solution. He arranged to pay the wardship by instalments[10], raising the money by selling off parts of the Fitz estate. Sir Alan describes the arrangement in a remarkable letter to his friend Dudley Carleton in October 1606, when Mary Fitz was just ten years old:

> My lord [his brother, the Earl of Northumberland] and I have met without any repetition of what was past, and has promised to pay that money for me, which I was a suitor to the King conditionally that I marry the ward. If I sell her, I must pay it back...[11]

Sir Alan's motives for the marriage were all too clear. Sir William Courtenay could do nothing to prevent large portions of land on the old Fitz estates, including Drake's Wood, being sold off by Sir Alan Percy to pay off his gambling debts. As Sir Alan rode around his new Devon estates, evaluating and considering what next to sell, the estate's stewards, Richard Halse and George Cutteford, were in a difficult position. Halse, still at nearby Walreddon Manor, must have been under considerable pressure to try to prevent any sales, but there was nothing he could do – the land belonged to Percy by his marriage to a twelve-year-old girl still in London, and he and George Cutteford were there merely to offer advice and prepare the appropriate papers.

---

10 Radford, 1890, p. 76.
11 Radford, 1890, p. 76.

However, the Percy family did not have long to enjoy their good fortune. In November 1611, whilst back in London, Alan Percy went out hunting, caught a cold and died. Death by common cold was not unusual at that time, and epidemics of influenza frequently killed hundreds. But it is strange that a wealthy man like Sir Alan did not recover. Perhaps the medicines in London were less effective than those in Tavistock. Certainly, Halse and Cutteford would have been delighted by the work of Sir Alan's physicians.

Sir Alan's death is curious, though. He caught something of a chill lying on the ground while hunting, but seemed well enough to everyone when he went to bed. Early the following morning, the 7 November, his friend Epsley was finally released from the Gatehouse prison, having been locked up on suspicion of some involvement with the Gunpowder Plot. Epsley immediately made for his brother's hunting lodge near Hackney, where Sir Alan was staying. Once there, Epsley was told his friend was still asleep, but on entering Sir Alan's chambers, Epsley found the poor man dead.[12]

Whatever the true cause of Sir Alan's passing, Mary, barely fifteen and now a widow, found herself immediately back on the market at the Court of Wards, with suitors lining up at Lady Hatton's house. Sadly, that same month, news of her mother's death reached Mary. The young girl must have been devastated, left so alone and acutely aware of the horror of her situation.

Some historians claim Mary then fell in love and escaped from Lady Hatton's house, in midwinter and in the dead of night, to elope with a young man called Thomas Darcy, who was then but sixteen. This would be a delightfully romantic tale if it were true. Mary was considered a great beauty, and a lively companion. Her running off into the night with a handsome young man is a lovely fairytale, but the story of the elopement has a disturbing twist. It seems that Mary may have been deliberately married off to a dying man.

---

12 Radford, 1890, p. 76.

Thomas Darcy's father was the 3rd Baron Darcy of Chichester. The Baron was faced with a dilemma. He had many daughters, but only one son, Thomas, who possibly became ill at fifteen years old, sometime in 1611 or 1612. Baron Darcy was already separated from his troublesome wife (or long-suffering, depending on whose side you were on). His wife was Mary Kytson, daughter and heir of Sir Thomas Kytson of Hengrave, and amongst her many daughters she gave Baron Darcy just one son. The hostile separation meant that the prospect of another legitimate son to replace Thomas as heir was limited. If Thomas died, the Baron and his family would lose not only his title, but all his property, including the grand manor and family home at St Osyth's, in Suffolk.[13] Baron Darcy urgently needed a healthy male heir, which meant finding a bride for Thomas.

At the moment Sir Alan Percy died, Mary became an ideal target for the Baron's attentions, now she was of marriageable and child-bearing age. How Baron Darcy procured Mary from Lady Hatton's house is still uncertain. It could be that he arranged an elopement, if that isn't a contradiction, or that he paid Sir Edmund Coke an appropriate fee to steal the girl away. Either way, Mary soon found herself in St Osyth's, under formidable pressure to have a child in a hurry.

Just a few months later, Thomas died, and was buried at the Kytson family's mausoleum in Hengrave Church. Mary's dilemma is immortalised in the engravings on Thomas' monument there:

Memoria sacrum
Of Thomas Darcy, here the body ly,
Only heire maile of Chiches Barony,
By Mary, heire of Kitson family.
With D'enshire Fitz's heire he wedded was,
But she from earth him issueless let pass.[14]

---

13 Watson, 1877.
14 Watson, 1877.

The Baron's devious plan had failed, and the house and all his titles were passed to his son-in-law, Sir Thomas Savage, married to the Baron's eldest daughter. In due course, Thomas Savage became Viscount Savage, with the title passing down to his sons and heirs, while the Barony of Darcy of Chich became extinct.

So Mary found herself twice widowed and somewhat disgraced by her failure to produce an heir in time, thereby destroying the Darcys' prospects. Mary was soon returned to Lady Hatton's house in London, like an uncompensated faulty gift. Lady Hatton must have felt sorry for the poor girl, and tried her best to find a more suitable match.

The many sons of the Earl of Suffolk, who were neighbours of the Darcy family, showed promise. The eldest boy, Theophilus, was the ideal candidate – but he had just married Elizabeth Home. The younger brother Thomas was considered, but he went on to marry Elizabeth Cecil in 1614.

Looking down the list of the remaining sons, Charles, just twenty-two and knighted that year, heir to the family's estates in Shropshire, seemed a very good candidate. The Howards were attracted to the prospect of a wealthy heiress. The Earl of Suffolk, struggling to finance his grand building plans, had just been forced to sell his London residence when Mary came onto the market.

In October 1612, Mary duly found herself married off to Sir Charles Howard and on her way to Audley End in Saffron Walden, now in Essex. As it would turn out, Lady Hatton had made a very poor choice.

THE HOWARDS OF SAFFRON WALDEN

The Earl of Suffolk, Charles Howard's father, had had a long career as a privateer. As Lord Thomas Howard, he had commanded the *Golden Lion* in the attack on the Spanish

Armada.[15] A favourite of Queen Elizabeth, he was sent with a fleet of ships in 1591 to the Azores to waylay the Spanish treasure fleets as they left America. His ship was one of the first to arrive at the Azores, and during the long wait for the remainder of his fleet he was forced to land to allow his sick men to recover and for repairs to be made. However, his ship were barely back in the water when they spotted a Spanish fleet approaching – not the few treasure ships they were expecting, but a substantial Spanish force that had been despatched to destroy Howard's fleet. Most of his fleet escaped just in time, all except the *Revenge*, captained by the fleet's Vice-Admiral, Sir Richard Grenville. Grenville's ship the *Revenge* was some distance from the other ships and decided to break through the Spanish forces, but after a long fight, Grenville was forced to surrender. The ship was destroyed and Grenville was mortally wounded in the fight, dying a hero's death and becoming a legend.

Subsequently, Howard fought in other successful privateering ventures, much to the favour of Queen Elizabeth, and was knighted, then created Baron Howard de Walden and subsequently Earl of Suffolk. Howard's finances were always in a perilous state, despite his support from Queen Elizabeth. He was a man who liked to spend money on land, good dowries for his daughters and extensive building programmes, including the construction of Audley End, his extensive palace near Saffron Walden, then in Suffolk, now in Essex. It was at that time the largest private house in England, and is now renowned as one of the finest Jacobean houses in England. The refurbishment was reputed to have cost £200,000 between 1603 and 1614.[16] King James himself stayed at the house twice, and joked

---

15 There are many excellent biographies of Lord Thomas Howard, 1st Earl of Suffolk. See Kate Jeffrey's book *Audley End* for English Heritage, 1997. Also the Wikipedia entry at: http://en.wikipedia.org/wiki/Thomas_Howard,_1st_Earl_of_Suffolk

16 Jeffrey, 1997, p. 30.

that the house was too large for a King, but it might do for a Lord Treasurer.

The Howard's fortunes would not last long. When James came to the throne, Thomas Howard was one of the few of Queen Elizabeth's favourites who seem to have managed to keep his position in court. In 1605, it was Thomas Howard who first examined the cellar under Parliament to uncover the Gunpowder Plot, and was one of those commissioned to investigate and try the plotters. In 1614, Thomas Howard inherited the Earl of Northampton's house at Charing Cross and began construction of an expensive new wing, while his wife set about building Charlton Park on the estates she had inherited. Thomas was appointed Lord High Treasurer the same year, a position that provided him with the opportunity to seek out the finances he needed, though his methods were not strictly legal.

The Earl of Suffolk then made the terrible mistake of trying to undermine the rising power of the Duke of Buckingham, favourite of the King, and Buckingham's revenge was absolute, referring Howard's financial misdealings to the King. In 1619, Thomas Howard and his wife were arrested, prosecuted, brutally humiliated in court, and found guilty on all counts of corruption. Imprisoned, they were forced to pay a fine of £30,000. They couldn't afford it.

Buckingham was magnanimous to his defeated rival and did manage to retrieve some of Thomas Howard's status, and his freedom; he then married off Howard's youngest son Edward to Buckingham's own niece to secure the deal. Thomas Howard, the Earl of Suffolk, never again rose to high office. He died in Charing Cross in London in 1626 and was buried near his precious estate at Saffron Walden.

———————

It is said that Mary married Charles Howard at Clun Castle on the Welsh borders. Charles had inherited the castle in Shropshire from his grandmother, so his full title was Sir

Charles Howard of Clun. Clun Castle itself was a ruin in the wilderness even in the seventeenth century, though it was probably seen as a romantic place for the wedding – at least, Charles was trying to start the marriage off with some fine sentiments. It wouldn't last.

On 21 September 1613, at Audley End, Mary had her first child, a girl called Elizabeth[17], but little more is heard of the girl subsequently and it is thought Elizabeth died very young. Her second daughter, Mary, was probably born at one of the Fitz houses in London, probably the grand house in Lewisham, south of the Thames.

It is uncertain when Mary first returned to Devon, but Charles was soon selling off large portions of woodland from her estates in Lewisham and Hornacot to fund his father's grand schemes.[18] Just like her first husband, Charles Howard was quick to survey her Devon estates with the prospects of further sales, requiring the assistance of her steward, George Cutteford, to do so. These were ominous portents.

By the time Mary returned to Fitzford, with Charles Howard, she already had a plan. Inspired by Lady Hatton's independence, and with the full support of her grandfather and the Courtenay family, she would soon reclaim control over all of the Fitz estates for herself. For her plan to succeed, however, she would require the full co-operation of the steward, George Cutteford. But how would she persuade him to co-operate?

---

17 Radford, 1890, p. 78
18 Radford, 1890, p. 78

Chapter Three

Revenge Served Cold

The woman who returned to Fitzford was a very different person from the nine-year-old girl who had been stolen away. Years of forced marriages and anxious separation from her family would have hardened the girl. Probably just seventeen as she re-entered the doors of Fitzford, with all its painful memories, she would have faced the marriage with a sense of foreboding – and with undeclared grievances. Charles could not have had any idea of the appalling events that would unfold.

Charles would have been very pleased with his first views of Fitzford. It was well situated on the edge of Tavistock, amongst

The parish church at Tavistock.

pretty meadows and encroaching forests. The woodlands alone were worth a fortune. What it lacked in manicured gardens and modern comforts was more than compensated by its views over the town and the moors beyond. It was a rural idyll that offered pastoral beauty.[1]

Neighbouring Walreddon Manor offered equal beauty and a significant income. Overlooking two river valleys, where the Walkham River joins the Tavy, known as Double Waters, Walreddon was well-placed within a thriving farming community, with extensive orchards and grazing lands on the edge of Dartmoor.

Walreddon was still occupied by Sir William Courtenay's agents, the Halses and their cousin George Cutteford. Riding out with Sir Charles Howard, George would have realised how privileged he was, in status and location, as steward of one of the largest estates in the country. Here he was successful, not just in his occupation. Having grown up in the overcrowded and noisy Plymouth docks, he was now bringing up his own family, not in the pitiful tenements of Tavistock, but in the ancient lands of Dartmoor.

There is a vastness distinctive to Dartmoor, a country of undulating hills and moors so far to the horizon that it can seem overwhelming in its emptiness. It has a primeval beauty still, lacking the aspirant decorations of the best of the fine houses, but instead fulfilling that simpler human desire to appreciate the earth as it is. Never mind the centuries of habitation that have forever changed the landscape; the mines, the farms, the wood-burning and wool that have cleared away the forests. Dartmoor is a land that retains its ancient authenticity, a heritage far older than even the Courtenay line.

---

[1]   There exists a wonderful image of the view of Tavistock from Fitzford, engraved after a picture by H. Worsley and published in History of Devonshire in 1830 (and reproduced on the website www.ancestryimages. com). Unfortunately, I know very little more about the image, but it shows an idyllic scene of meadows and pastures overlooking the spire of the parish church.

In seventeenth-century England, ownership of land, the accumulation of acreage, and the splendid structures placed upon it – these were the measure of success. Land was power, influence, the future. Land mattered.

George Cutteford knew all too well the value of land and property. Surveying the Fitz estates with Charles Howard, George would have held secret ambitions to acquire some of that wealth for his family, to become a landowner instead of a land-agent. To be able to bequeath some of that ancient land to his sons became his new objective. Oblivious to his steward's ambitions, Sir Charles Howard was probably delighted that his new wife had brought him such fine assets.

But what of Mary Howard? Before she was twenty, she had been twice widowed, thrice married, and twice a mother, already grieving the death of her first child. She had experienced and suffered more in ten years than most people endured in a lifetime. With both parents dead, her old acquaintance George Cutteford was the only steady influence in her life – and she clung to him like a drowning child.

Now as a grown woman, she was attractive, flirtatious, clever and manipulative when she wanted to be. George Cutteford found himself not only attracted to the Fitz estates, but also to his employer's wife. Initially, he refused her advances, acutely aware that he was a man of low status, with his own wife and children to consider.

Between 1605 and Mary's return to Fitzford, sometime in 1614, George Cutteford had established himself as an attorney in an increasingly Puritan community. George's wife Grace found her allegiance lay with the Puritan values of Tavistock. Her religious views would, it seems, slowly alienate her husband, while George's growing attraction to the young Mary Howard would tear him away from his jealous wife.

In the meantime, the Cuttefords would have five children: Eleanor, George, Grace, John and Anne, the eldest boy probably born around 1607 while Mary was still in London. It is possible that George and his family were still living with their Halse cousins at Walreddon, while George worked with Richard Halse to oversee the many Fitz family estates.

George Cutteford's position meant his daughters would marry well. Eleanor married John Skerrit, a successful local man, probably a farmer. Grace married one of the Radfords from Whitchurch, while Anne found herself married to Thomas Robinson, the land agent and sometimes business partner of the Earl of Dorset.[2]

Before the arrival of the Howards, Cutteford and his family lived in relative peace in the Tavistock community, regularly worshipping at one of the many meeting houses, slowly improving their lives and planning their futures amidst progressive ideas of non-conformity and Puritan thinking. Mary's return would destroy it all.

TAVISTOCK IN THE EARLY SEVENTEENTH CENTURY

Tavistock had a long history of non-conformity in religious matters. The 2nd Earl of Bedford and Marquess of Tavistock, Sir Francis Russell, was an ardent supporter of religious reform, and the Russell family continued their support of Puritan thinking for many generations, and throughout the English Civil War, though it is unlikely Sir Francis Russell ever lived in Tavistock. The Russell family had an estate at Woburn Abbey, north of Oxford, and had been awarded the old Abbey at Tavistock at the time of the Dissolution of the Monasteries in the mid-1500s, and their fortunes had prospered.[3]

---

2 See documents SAS/G23/5 and SAS/G23/34, from 1618 and 1625 respectively, held at East Sussex Record Office, for details of Thomas Robinson's employment by Edward Sackville, Earl of Dorset.

3 UK Geneaology Archives notes the inheritance of the Earl of Bedford, at http://uk-genealogy.org.uk/england/Devon/towns/Tavistock.html. I also highly recommend the entertaining stories of Mrs Bray, including her 1838 book on the traditions and history of Devonshire. See Bray, p. 97.

In 1612, the Earl of Bedford granted the vicarage at
Tavistock to Edward Eliott, preacher of God's word[4],
encouraging Puritan views which would continue with
subsequent appointments, including the able Puritan
George Hughes, Bachelor of Divinity, in 1638. Hughes,
as lecturer at All Hallows in London, had been literally
silenced by Archbishop Laud, in Laud's attempts to attack
the rise of Puritan preachers, making Hughes an ideal candidate for the Tavistock post. Hughes in turn would inspire
the conversion of Ralph Venning, who became a celebrated
Puritan preacher and writer; his works of devotion would
run to many editions. Hughes would also inspire his son-
in-law, the celebrated Puritan divine, John Howe. The tides
turned on them all, however, when, in 1662, King Charles
II ordered a final purge of Puritan preachers, and Hughes,
Venning and Howe were all ejected from their ministries.

The famous adventurer Sir Francis Drake, born and
raised in Tavistock, his father a preacher, had also supported
religious reforms. George Cutteford's family friends, the
Maynards, were Presbyterians. The schools established by
the Maynards and their associate Elize Hele were at the
time non-conformist and independent of the Catholic or
Church of England faiths.[5]

George's cousin Richard Halse had married the daughter
of the Bishop of Exeter, Dr Matthew Sutcliffe, renowned
for his controversial writings, demanding reforms in the
church and attacking any signs of Catholic rituals. Amongst
the Tavistock Puritans, the papist rituals, Church hierarchies
and luxurious decor of the Catholic Church were unwel-
come in their simple and unadorned meeting houses.

However, in 1613, Tavistock was a failing economy. Once
the location for Henry VIII's Council of the West, then a
major Stannary town under Queen Elizabeth I, its tin

---

4   Alford, 1891.

5   The Maynard's School survives in Exeter, the third oldest girls' school in
    Britain. Hele's School is still in Plympton.

mines were ailing and its fortunes fading under King James
I. (Tin mining would flourish again only when the indus-
trial machinery could reach the deeper reserves.) The cloth
manufacturing industry alone kept Tavistock afloat during
the difficult years.[6]

Politically too, the town was ailing. Sir Francis Glanville, a
wealthy local landowner whose family had made money from
the tanning industry, was supposed to represent Tavistock in
Parliament, but King James I was never impressed by the
concept of a 'Parliament' which repeatedly refused to pay off
his increasing debts. James therefore called Parliament only
a few times in the early seventeenth century and Glanville's
position in the 'Addled Parliament' of 1614 lasted barely a
few weeks before it was again dissolved by King James.

Tavistock remained unnoticed and unrepresented, feeling
rejected and frequently at odds with King James's pronouncements about the Divine Right of Kings, religious
conformity, and his demands for more and more taxes to
support his expensive lifestyle.

———————————

Charles Howard's arrival caused quite a stir for the people
of Tavistock. The Howard family were known to be Catholics,
although they tended to keep their religious views to themselves, fearing the wrath of successive Protestant monarchs.
Charles Howard was also the son of a privateer; his father
was famed for his ostentatious spending and unruly behaviour, drinking and womanising being the least of his sins.
Charles soon demonstrated a love of gambling and drinking,
and the locals must have been worried that they had another
'John Fitz' come to terrorise the neighbourhood, but it seems
that Charles Howard was a gentleman who terrorised no one.

Perhaps they thought the arrival of Sir Charles Howard of
Clun to oversee the restoration of the old Fitz estates would

———————————

6   Woodcock, 2008.

help the fortunes of the ailing town? Charles Howard was, after all, the son of one of the Lords of the Treasury, financial mis-dealings aside. Perhaps Charles would have the intelligence and knowledge to turn the town's fortunes around and increase prosperity for everyone?

Sadly, he didn't.

Sir William Courtenay's own disquiet about the Howards had nothing to do with religion or local economics. If Mary's marriage to Charles Howard was successful – if she bore him a son – the Fitz fortune, once entailed to Mary's mother Bridget, was lost to the Courtenays forever. If Charles Howard had a son, Sir William could lose all claim over his daughter's (and now grand-daughter's) inheritance. But how was he to prevent a young married couple having a son? In time, it was his agent George Cutteford who would provide an unusual solution.

George Cutteford was probably ordered to ingratiate himself into the new household, and report any developments back to Richard Halse, who would in turn keep Sir William informed. Cutteford's first priority would be to keep the estates together and solvent, as much as possible, though Mary never did pay off her wardship fees to the Court of Wards. It is possible that Mary simply withheld them out of spite.

Though there is no written record of George Cutteford's feelings towards Mary at the time, he must have felt sorry for this young woman sorely used by the Court of Wards, auctioned off to suitor after suitor. Indeed, a friendship seems to have blossomed between the pair, despite their very different status and backgrounds – a friendship that would not normally have been accepted by society of the seventeenth century, where social hierarchies were strictly maintained and defended. (Even clothing was determined by status, with strict punishments for transgressors.) George Cutteford was only the son of a sailor. Marriage to a customs officer's daughter improved his standing, but he was still of a much lower class than the wife of Sir Charles Howard. It was a friendship, though, that was apparently never discouraged by Sir William Courtenay or the Halses.

Sir William's plans to recover the estate from the Howards were to face a major hurdle. For all his Puritan background and education, George discovered that this young man, Charles Howard, this son of a privateer, was a difficult man not to like. Charles was very much a Howard; he enjoyed his drinking and his gambling, but not in a destructive manner – or at least, not at first – and was a gentleman of good standing who enjoyed social gatherings.

In turn, Charles became a good friend to George Cutteford. He invited George to meet the rest of the Howard family at their palatial homes in London and Saffron Walden and George was welcomed not as a servant – or even as an estate manager – but as a friend. How different the Howard lifestyle must have seemed to this man used to organising contracts for the lowly tenement buildings in ailing Tavistock, working as an associate of Richard Halse. Suddenly he found himself invited to lavish balls and hunting parties, standing alongside the wealthy and extravagant Howards. Theophilus Howard, eldest son of the Earl of Suffolk and heir to the estate, along with his cousin, the Earl of Dorset, would remain George's good friends for life. In time, Dorset's land agent, Thomas Robinson, would marry Anne Cutteford, George's daughter.[7]

Arriving in the extensive and manicured gardens of Audley End in Saffron Walden, George Cutteford's eyes must have been opened to a new way of life, a life of wealth and status he had never really experienced before; certainly not anything imagined by his parents struggling to live in their two-room apartment in a sailors' tenement in Plymouth. Away from the Puritanical views of his wife, George enjoyed himself. Moreover, he realised that a better future lay in store for his

---

7   See documents SAS/G23/5 and SAS/G23/34, from 1618 and 1625 respectively, held at East Sussex Record Office, for details of Thomas Robinson's employment by Edward Sackville, Earl of Dorset. Also see PROB 11/285, the will of George Cutteford the younger, originally written in 1646 and held at the National Archives, for details of Anne's marriage to Thomas Robinson.

children, if he could only make good use of these new connections. With the Howards and the Earl of Dorset as friends,
the future for George Cutteford's family looked very good
indeed.

In the early days of the marriage, Mary seems to have
found some happiness too. The Howards were always very
kind to her, and she enjoyed their grand and gracious lifestyle.
The extravagant parties and social gatherings were ideal
opportunities for her to display her charms – she was beautiful,
bright, though not demonstrably too intelligent for a woman
of her class, and, according to the historians, a notorious flirt.

Charles' father, the Earl of Suffolk, saw Mary as a welcome
source of income. His excessive spending, his lavish building
programme and the costs and subsequent failures of his investments in the first colonies in the New World[8] would soon out-
strip his income, so the money coming from all the Fitz estates,
carefully managed by the amiable George Cutteford, was very
welcome indeed.

The Earl of Suffolk was the King's Lord High Treasurer
and used his status to embezzle a little money for himself,
but when he was caught by the King's favourite, the Duke
of Buckingham, his elaborate lifestyle suddenly soured. In
October 1619, he found himself in prison and unable to pay
the heavy fines imposed.

This was the moment Sir William Courtenay had been
waiting for. Charles Howard's father was suddenly facing a
fine of £30,000, a phenomenal sum, and Charles was under
considerable pressure to provide funds to pay the fine. It
seemed that the Fitz estates would have to be sold off, piece

---

8　The Earl of Suffolk and his eldest son Theophilus are listed as two of the
hundreds of investors in the first colonies in North America, established by
King James I. The investors came from all walks of life, from gentry to shop-
keepers. The initial colonies failed, however, the investors losing their money.
Just as the colonies started to return on their investments, King James I re-
claimed all the land as belonging to the Crown and most investors never saw
their money again; another reason for many people to be unhappy with the
monarchy.

by piece. Mary was horrified. She was a canny business
woman herself, though she seems to have kept her own abilities at managing the estate a secret from Charles. He certainly
never suspected that she had ambitions to keep the estate
together by any means necessary. Mary knew her business
better than Charles. She was determined to save her inheritance. Her grandfather, Sir William Courtenay, would eagerly
come to the rescue.

Sir William suggested that he pay the Earl of Suffolk's fine,
with some assistance from the Earl of Pembroke, another of
James I's favourite courtiers; in return, Charles would hand the
Fitz estates over to their keeping.[9] Charles reluctantly agreed
and the Earl of Pembroke and Sir William Courtenay became
trustees of all the Fitz estates, with Sir William's grand-
daughter Mary retaining a life interest in them. Charles was
permitted to cut and sell timber, which he continued to do,
but the estates were now finally back in the hands of the tri-
umphant Sir William Courtenay.

Within months, Charles left Fitzford. Perhaps he was needed
by his family in London; perhaps he wished to escape the
gloating Sir William Courtenay. Some blame the behaviour
of his wife, whose reputation for flirting caused him much
embarrassment. She showed, it is said, an amorous interest in
every handsome man she met – including her husband's dear
friend George Cutteford.

Of course, Charles would never consider a man like
George Cutteford to be any real threat. George was a sensible,
responsible man, and, although raised in status by friendship,
he was sure that George knew his place in the scheme of
things. He was still the son of a sailor, not even qualified as

---

9   See Radford, p.78. In October 1619, the Fitz estates were transferred to Sir
    William Courtney and the Earl of Pembroke (and also his brother, the Earl of
    Montgomery). Many relating the story of Mary Howard blame Mary's disrep-
    utable behaviour as the primary cause of Charles relinquishing the estate, but
    forget that at the very same time, the Howards were urgently raising money
    to pay off the Earl of Suffolk's enormous fine.

a lawyer, so his employer's wife would certainly be out of bounds. To Charles' eyes, George was seemingly content in his occupation, his status, and his marriage. He certainly gave the appearance of being a happy family man, ambitious for his children, but not prone to immoral behaviour. George's Puritan and charitable upbringing would surely deny him such temptations. Charles may even have laughed at the idea of his wife seducing the steward. Everyone presumed that nothing would come of the flirtation.

By 1620, Charles and Mary Howard had formally separated and Charles departed Tavistock in disgrace. He had lost his family's claim to the Fitz properties, his father was ruined, and the rumours of his wife's amorous liaisons spread far and wide. In the seventeenth century, a man could commit adultery and not lose his reputation – success with women was actually seen to increase his reputation. However, if a man's wife strayed, his reputation was in ruins. Sometimes a husband would charge his wife with adultery – and the punishments on women were horrific – but the embarrassment attending such cases frequently prevented them from reaching a court.

Charles, to his credit, seems to have left quietly, with little if any fuss. He knew when he was beaten. Some say that he spent subsequent years travelling in Europe[10] though this is unlikely, with the Thirty Years War still raging. Of course, Charles may possibly have joined Horace Vere's regiment heading to the battlefields in 1620; he certainly spent some time dealing with Howard family business in London, trying to live down the humiliation he had suffered.

Mary was probably pleased to see Charles go. Though the estate was officially in trust to her grandfather, she now controlled quite an empire, making her one of the wealthiest women in the country – and she had some plans of her own that she was about to put into action.

---

10 Miller, 1979.

Within months of Charles leaving, Mary invited George Cutteford to live with her at Fitzford.[11] She was then twenty-four; he was probably in his forties. Their affair had possibly started months before. With Charles' departure, they could at last be together.

Over a number of years, George's experiences with the Howard family had estranged him from his wife. Suddenly he found the courage to leave her. Together, Mary and George ran the estate, though their relationship was somehow kept a secret from the public. George's wife Grace did not make a fuss, though the income George was making from the Fitz estates would have been some compensation. Perhaps she thought her husband would soon be home again; wives in the seventeenth century were not ones to complain – or at least not in public. Mary's relatives have left no record of complaint either – perhaps they too did not see George Cutteford as a threat. They now had the Fitz estates, and there was nothing George could do that would be a danger to those arrangements. It is possible that Mary and George managed to keep their relationship a secret from everyone, but it seems highly unlikely. Gossip was one of the few entertainments of the time, so the secret could not be kept long – especially after Mary gave birth to George Cutteford's son.

The birth of their child would prove to be a momentous occasion for everyone.

---

11 Miller, 1979, also Radford, 1890.

Chapter Four

An Heir Apparent

I n 1622, Mary gave birth to a son and called him George. Everyone in Tavistock would have known he was not the child of Charles Howard. Sir Charles had been away at least eighteen months before the child was born, and naming the baby George did nothing to dispel the rumours.

JAMES I *King of Great Britain,*
France & Ireland, &c

James I. (Courtesy of the Library of Congress, Prints & Photographs Division, LC-USZ62-104640)

ILLICIT LIAISONS

In the seventeenth century, having a child outside of marriage could mean disaster, particularly for women. Punishments against such immorality were brutally severe.

In Bideford, a young girl became pregnant by her suitor, with sickening consequences. Her mother had allowed the engaged couple to live together in the family house, expecting a wedding any day. But the suitor, on hearing the news of the baby to come, panicked and ran, leaving the poor girl unmarried and pregnant. The court's punishment was severe: the deserted young girl of about fifteen was paraded through the town and whipped in the town square.[1]

This type of punishment was not restricted to the lower classes. Frances Coke, the poor daughter of Lady Hatton who had been forced to marry John Villiers, found herself falling in love with Robert Howard (by odd coincidence, the older brother of Mary's husband Charles Howard[2]). With John Villiers growing increasingly deranged, Frances spent her time in clandestine liaisons with her lover and eventually became pregnant. The Villiers family determined that the child could not be that of her husband as John was under severe restraint at the time to prevent him from harming himself. So Frances and Robert Howard were brought before the Court of High Commission and condemned to public penance.

Fortunately for Robert, Charles I had just come to the throne, and gave Robert a Coronation pardon. Frances was not so fortunate. She was required to pay a fine of £500 and condemned to walk barefoot, on a Sunday, from St Paul's Cross (near the Cathedral in London) to the door of the Savoy Chapel near the Strand. If that wasn't bad

---

1   Gowing, 1996.
2   Fraser, 1984.

enough, she was required to wear only a white sheet and stand at the chapel door for all to see. Frances managed to escape, cleverly dressed as a page-boy. She and her lover fled to France, returning many years later, after the Duke of Buckingham, her brother-in-law, had been assassinated. Sadly for her, the old warrant was still enforced and Frances found herself imprisoned once more in the Westminster prison called the Gatehouse. Conditions there were appalling, but, undaunted, she paid off the gaoler and made her escape again. This time she had to travel alone to France, as Sir Robert was now incarcerated and only released on the promise that he would never see Frances again. Once free, he immediately broke his promise and sought out his lover in France. The King's officials followed them, stubbornly determined to see justice done, and Frances was forced into a nunnery to hide, eventually dying in penury and never realising her inheritance.

Lacking any reliable forms of contraception, illegitimate children were quite common in seventeenth-century society. But because of such severe punishments, it was rare for anyone to bring them to the law's attention; no one relished seeing their friends or neighbours prosecuted, even if the child was the result of immoral behaviour. So communities were full of 'hidden' children, with the mothers giving birth in secrecy and the children frequently brought up by grandmothers or married sisters.

Mary and George were determined to avoid prosecution for adultery. Before their baby was due, Mary hid away in the quiet seclusion of Walreddon, in the care of the Halses, her grandfather's agents. The child was then brought up as though he was the son of Ann Halse, Richard Halse's wife. Ann would have had to undergo the rituals of 'veiling', compulsory for new mothers (*see* 'The Rituals of Childbirth'), in place of Mary, but that may have publicly persuaded the local population of the boy's parentage and Mary's innocence. With gossiping servants around, everyone would have known the truth of the baby's birth, but at least Anne Halse's veiling created a socially acceptable lie. The boy was subsequently baptised George Halse, and Mary and her lover escaped prosecution.

There is also a sense that George Cutteford was well-liked in the community, born out by subsequent events. Admired for his honesty as well as his legal advice, no one wanted to see him prosecuted. So the secret was kept by everyone, and George Halse spent his first year hidden away at Walreddon.

THE RITUALS OF CHILDBIRTH

Having a baby in seventeenth-century England was a precarious endeavour[3]. The mother, if she survived the traumas of labour, was expected to remain in the same sheets in the birthing room, usually her bed chamber, for forty days after the baby was born, even if the baby did not survive. This was an age-old means of preventing infection, which was a mortal threat to the newborn and the mother. Many women complained about this imprisonment, with some justification – it must have been a horrible and claustrophobic experience to be trapped in the mess and the smell after giving birth. Women of the day put forward an argument that they should still be allowed to attend church, which was compulsory for everyone for the sake of their immortal souls.

The midwives then came up with a novel solution: women would be permitted to leave the birthing room to attend church, but only if they wore a white veil over their faces and sat in a special chair laid on in the church just for them. The veil was a sensible barrier to prevent new mothers catching diseases from anyone coughing around them. For a society apparently ignorant of the existence of bacteria or

---

3   Purkiss, 2006.

viruses, the midwives seemed surprisingly aware of them, and the means of transmitting disease. It would be many years before medicine caught up with their knowledge and experience.

But, typically of the times, these sensible arrangements were explained to new mothers in damning terms by the priests. Mothers were declared to be soiled by the sins of Eve, which could contaminate the souls of anyone who came into contact with them, even by their breathing on them – hence the veil. The birthing blood of a new mother was seen as a vile fluid, filled with transferrable sin, and no one else should have to be in contact with it, hence the special chair. The veil became a symbol of the biblical sin of womenfolk, and was subsequently despised by women of the seventeenth century. Sadly, what started as a sensible hygienic precaution to save the lives of new mothers and their babies led to women's voices raised in protest against a ritual which turned new mothers in social outcasts.

Previously it was thought that George Cutteford had hidden the child, taking the newborn baby to his mother's house[4], but his mother Ann, if still alive in 1622, was too old to care for a baby. Life with a sailor's widow in Plymouth would have been considered most unsuitable for the great grandson of Sir William Courtenay. The Halses at Walreddon were a more suitable alternative.

However, it seems that the boy's situation was still precarious. Perhaps the Halses were worried that Charles would return; perhaps local gossip continued; or perhaps they just waited until the boy was old enough to travel – travelling with a newborn was a difficult and often dangerous prospect on the terrible roads of the seventeenth century. Whatever the reason, in 1623 the Halses suddenly quit Walreddon, hand-

---

4   Miller, 1979.

ing the entire estate over to the delighted Frances Glanville, still acting as MP for Tavistock. The Halses returned to their Kenedon Manor, at Kenton near Exmouth, taking the now twelve-month-old George Halse with them.

It is possible that Richard Halse and his family simply wished to return to the family estate. Perhaps he was recalled by Sir William Courtenay, who no longer needed his watchful eye on the Mary's estate. Possibly Sir William Courtenay was concerned that the Howard's might claim the boy as their own and re-ignite the battle for ownership of the estate. Sir William was by then in his seventies, and had not been active in Parliament since 1601. Francis Courtenay, his son and heir, now in his forties, had taken over the running of the Powderham estates. By 1626, he would be a very powerful man, appointed Lord Warden of the Stannaries. Francis' first wife remained childless, so there was still the worrying lack of an heir. Perhaps it was Francis who decided that Mary's illegitimate child should be safely hidden away nearby, with the Halses at Kenedon. However, wherever he was, George Halse would not remain hidden for long.

Charles Howard was still alive and well. The fines on his father that had driven him out of the estate had just been reduced by the king from £30,000 to just £8,000 – so he could easily argue that the money offered by Sir William Courtenay was no longer necessary, and reclaim the Fitz estates. The Courtenay's claim was suddenly quite tenuous. Meanwhile, George Cutteford remained at Fitzford with Mary. The departure of their son to Kenedon must have been very upsetting, and Mary's actions later in life would reveal that she never forgave the Halses for stealing away her beloved boy. Of course, in 1623, she was in an impossible position: if she protested, she would be prosecuted and perhaps imprisoned for adultery and the boy would probably be taken anyway. If the Howards discovered the existence of the child, they could quite easily say he was Charles' heir and re-claim the entire Fitz estate for themselves.

To make matters worse, Charles Howard did return to Tavistock. In May 1626, his father, the Earl of Suffolk, died at Charing Cross House in London. He was sixty-four and probably never fully recovered from his imprisonment. His grieving family arranged for his body to be taken back to his palatial estate in Saffron Walden for burial, and Charles returned from his travels to attend the funeral. Charles' elder brother, Theophilus Howard, inherited the title as the 2nd Earl of Suffolk, along with crippling debts, and it was probably Theophilus who convinced Charles that now would be a good time to return to Devon and claim his fair share of the Fitz estates.

Charles was in for a surprise. He returned to the Fitz manor to discover his wife living with his steward, George Cutteford. Charles' daughter Mary was still living with them, all seemingly as a happy if unusual family, and, to make matters worse, there was a rumour circulating that Mary and George had had a son – now a possible heir to the entire estate. Charles' reaction is unfortunately lost to history, but it can't have been a pleasant homecoming.

And then an unexpected resolution of Mary's predicament: Sir Charles Howard died.[5] Soon after he arrived in Tavistock in 1626, Charles was dead – yet another death in strange circumstances linked to the Fitz estate.

Some say he committed suicide, overcome by melancholy once confronted by the true extent of his wife's infidelity – but this seems improbable considering his previous behaviour. Perhaps his unexpected arrival turned to violent confrontation, and Charles was somehow killed in the affray. Later in life, Mary would, they say, display a chilling ability to remove those who got in her way, by any means necessary, so perhaps Mary ordered someone to kill her unfortunate husband.

---

5   The recorded date of the death of Sir Charles Howard seems to vary, with Mrs Radford in 1890 recording his death as early as September 1622. Mrs Radford could be correct, as she consulted many of the Whitchurch parish records. If Charles did die in 1622, just after the birth of Mary's illegitimate child, then the cause of his death becomes even more mysterious.

There is another possible explanation, however. In 1626, plague raged through Tavistock, and hundreds died. Of the no more than 4,000 inhabitants, 575 were buried that year, 331 of them in the months of August, September and October, just as Charles was arriving in the town.[6] It is possible that Charles contracted the terrible disease. However, the wealthy of the seventeenth century did have an uncanny knack of avoiding the plague. Despite the lack of medical knowledge, it was all too apparent that the best way to avoid the plague was to stay away from anyone who was poor and living in atrocious housing conditions. The rich regularly managed to leave town until the disease burnt itself out.

So Sir Charles Howard was dead, at the age of just thirty-six, and Mary was again a widow. Her son George Halse was safe with relatives at Kenedon, and remained undetected, and there was no reason for the Howards to contest the ownership of the Fitz estates. The Fitz estates were now safely in the hands of the Courtenays. George Cutteford seems to have been alone in his disquiet. He should have been a happy man, but Charles's death brought him feelings only of guilt and remorse. Charles had been a good friend to George and his family, after all. This guilt seems to have worked upon George's feelings, for by the end of 1626 Cutteford had left Mary Howard and returned to his wife and family, who may have returned to their old home in Plympton St Mary. George settled back into a steady life as an attorney and a good family man.

The money he acquired during his relationship with Mary certainly benefited his family – his eldest son, George, was already studying at Exeter College in Oxford.[7] In January 1628, George Cutteford the younger received a house called Tuddybrooke in Whitchurch.[8] Tuddybrooke was adjacent to the Walreddon estates; an area now called Tiddy Brook with a housing estate located there called Tiddy Close, next to a

6   Woodcock, 2008, and Alford, 1891.

7   Add Ms 18008 -771, 1628. Held at West Sussex Record Office.

8   Add Ms 18008 -771, 1628. Held at West Sussex Record Office.

retail park, probably on the land once owned by the younger George Cutteford. Nearby Brook Mill, which serviced the Walreddon and adjoining estates, still exists.

Meanwhile, Mary must have been devastated by the elder George Cutteford's departure. George was the only steady influence she had had all her life. Her closest friend was gone. Yet again she was a widow, and George was no longer there to support her. However, Mary Howard didn't stay unhappy for long. She did what any spurned lover would do; what any woman would do who found herself heartbroken and suddenly alone – she sued her brother-in law. She packed her bags and left for London with a couple of servants, and probably her daughter Mary in tow, and took Theophilus Howard to court.

On her marriage to Charles, the Howard family had established a jointure for Mary which would provide her with a widow's pension of £600 a year in the event of Charles's death.[9] When Charles died, however, the property they had set aside was not bringing in anything like the £600 they promised, so Mary took the matter to court.[10]

WOMEN IN COURT

It may seem unusual for a woman of the seventeenth century to stand up for herself in court, but in fact the Chancery Court at the time was filled with the cases of widows arguing for improved pensions and on behalf of the estates of their late husbands.[11] Women were not passive in their acceptance of their sorry lot – far from it. What prevented them from travelling to London to appear in court were usually domestic matters, such as the overwhelming

---

9 Miller, 1979, pp. 23 and 24, and Radford, 1890, p. 79.

10 Miller, 1979, pp. 23 and 24, and Radford, 1890, p. 79.

11 Stretton, 1998. An excellent study of women's involvement in legal cases, though Stretton does not always stress the limitations of child-rearing at the time.

demands of repeated pregnancies and childcare and the very real dangers of travelling alone.

Fathers, brothers and husbands were expected to represent their female relatives' interests in court, frequently forced into doing so by very strong-willed women, taking with them to London strict instructions to ensure the matter was decided in the women's favour. Women of the time were not shy in their demands, nor were they ignorant of legal matters, despite their lack of formal education. Widows, now released from the burden of childcare and other domestic responsibilities, were frequently to be found arguing their case in the London courts.

The rapid social changes of the early seventeenth century were promising great improvements in the rights of women. By the 1640s, women were demanding, amongst other things, equal rights in marriage and inheritance, improved child care and, heaven forbid, a say in how the country was governed.[12] Sadly, the outcome of the English Civil War would destroy all of that.[13]

———————

Under the circumstances, with Charles having being so sorely used by his faithless wife, and having died an untimely death, Mary's actions against the Howards may seem very inappropriate, but Mary was not one to let propriety and sympathy for the still-grieving Theophilus stand in her way. In 1627, Mary saw her case against Theophilus Howard as her opportunity to stand up for herself. At the same time, she also sued William Counton, who had purchased some woodland near her Lewisham Estate from her late husband – now the land was officially hers again, Mary wanted it all back.[14]

———————

12 Davies, 1999, gives an excellent account of women and protest in seventeenth-century England.

13 Davies, 1999.

14 Radford, 1890, p. 79, mentions Lady Howard's suit against William Counton and William Foster, who had purchased lands from Sir Charles Howard.

There was also the attraction of a new life for this widow of extremely independent means. The court of King Charles I was an exciting place for a woman who was free to choose her own friends – and probably a few lovers as well.[15] Her old friend and cousin, the Earl of Dorset, was Lord Chamberlain to the Queen and with such connections, Mary quickly became a favourite of Queen Henrietta Maria who, like the Howards, enjoyed lavish social gatherings and theatrical entertainments.

KING CHARLES I

Charles (1600-1649) was the second son of King James I. His elder and more popular brother Henry died of suspected typhoid in 1612, leaving the sickly Charles as heir to the throne. Charles' sister married Prince Frederick V, who was a Protestant, contesting the throne of Bohemia against the unpopular King Ferdinand II, a Catholic, resulting in the brutal turmoil of the Thirty Years War.

James I supported his son-in-law Frederick, and tried to make peace between Catholics and Protestants by marrying Charles to a Catholic princess from Spain, despite complaints from his own Protestant Parliament.

Parliament eventually approved Charles' marriage to the Catholic princess, Henrietta Maria of France, on condition that Roman Catholics outside Henrietta's court were not afforded any liberty of religion. Unknown to Parliament, however, King James entered into a treaty with Henrietta's father to aid the French in their violent suppression of the Protestant Huguenots at La Rochelle. The people of England were horrified to discover King James I supporting Catholicism, but Charles' marriage went ahead

---

15 Fraser, 1984, pp. 82-84, gives wonderful examples of the freedom women found in widowhood. Also Tinniswood, 2007, shows the family's consternation caused by a 'free-thinking' widow.

anyway after the death of King James and before Charles called his first Parliament – they certainly would have banned the wedding.

Parliament and the people distrusted the marriage, Henrietta Maria's luxurious lifestyle and her strong influence over the monarchy, with Charles demanding changes to the rituals of the Church of England that seemed Catholic in nature, in direct opposition to the rise in Puritan thinking. Religious differences alienated Charles from his Parliament, becoming one of the major causes of the English Civil War in 1642.

Meanwhile, the Thirty Years War was consuming Europe, and Charles demanded money from Parliament to take English forces into Spain to support his Protestant brother-in-law. England's finances were still suffering from the profligate reign of James I, so Parliament refused. Charles then raised the money through unpopular taxes, and sent his armies, led by court favourite the Duke of Buckingham, into disastrous battles. Ironically, the aim of one of these battles led by Buckingham was to protect the Huguenots, with Charles reneging on his treaty with his father-in-law the King of France. Its failure furthered Parliament's hatred of the Duke of Buckingham, who was subsequently assassinated by a disgruntled soldier on 23 August 1628.

Charles continued in his father's resolute belief in the Divine Right of Kings, stating that the liberty and freedom of the people meant they had a government, but not necessarily a share in the powers of that government. His continued battles with Parliament over power and authority – in particular that the laws of *habeas corpus* did not apply to the monarch – led to his eventual execution as authorised by the head of Parliament's army, Oliver Cromwell. Charles was beheaded at Whitehall on 30 January 1649. In an unusual act, Cromwell ordered Charles' head be sewn back onto his body, so that the family could pay their respects.[16]

───────────────

While enjoying herself in London, Mary had her portrait painted by Van Dyke[17], and although only a copied etching from 1657 survives, it shows Mary living a fine life, with no sign of heartbreak or loneliness. Mary is looking a bit plump as she enters her thirties, and the etching is not flattering in its detail – the style of her mouth, unnaturally small, is an affectation of the portrait styles of the day, indicating how women even in the seventeenth century would have their images 'airbrushed' to suit the fashion. There are, however, still signs of a surviving beauty.

A copy might have been sent to George Cutteford to remind him of just what he had lost. Certainly, there is something in her eyes that suggests a hardened disapproval of the viewer. Despite the curls and curves, there is nothing soft about this woman.

While at court, Mary attracted the attentions of the Duke of Buckingham, who had become a favourite of King Charles and was now just as influential as he had been in the court of King James. Charles sorely missed his elder brother, Henry[18], whom he had worshipped, and the Duke of Buckingham, this good-looking man of action and intellect, became a welcome replacement.

Mary Howard was flattered by the attentions of the Duke. Buckingham had a good friend he wanted Mary to meet,

───────────────

16   See the Wikipedia page for an example of the telling of this story: http://en.wikipedia.org/wiki/Charles_I_of_England#Execution

17   Radford, 1890, p. 79. Van Dyke's original portrait seems to have been lost, but in early catalogues of Hollar's work the image is called Lady Howard. The original must have been painted before 1641, when Van Dyke died. It has since been attributed to Lady Catherine Howard and Lady Venetia Digby, but, according to Mrs Radford, other images of these ladies look entirely different. It is therefore generally accepted as a copy of a painting of Lady Mary Howard.

18   . Henry, Prince of Wales, favourite son of King James I, died when he was eighteen years old, his death thought to have been caused by typhoid fever.

a man who would offer Mary assistance in her battles in court against Theophilus Howard, now the 2nd Earl of Suffolk. Buckingham was delighted to support any case against his old adversaries the Howards, and this friend of his was an adventurous man who had fought alongside Buckingham in Spain and France; a handsome man of good breeding and social standing, with a remarkable combination of wit and virility, a man who was secretly in need of a good marriage to pay back his many creditors. A man called Sir Richard Grenville.

When she first met the dashing Sir Richard Grenville, Mary fell instantly in love.

Chapter Five

The Devil Comes to Dartmoor

Sometime in 1628, George Cutteford was ordered to report to Richard Halse at Kenedon.[1] The news Halse relayed to his nephew was terrible: Mary Howard had decided, without consulting any of her family, to marry again. Nothing, it seemed, would dissuade her. She was determined to marry Sir Richard Grenville, much to the disapproval of Sir William Courtenay, who knew this suitor only too well. Sir Richard was known to be a decadent spendthrift, a disgrace to the Grenville family – he already owed Sir William money, with no sign of paying it back. He was certainly not the kind of man who should be allowed to inherit Mary's interest in the Fitz estates.

Charles I.

George Cutteford was instructed to do something about it. He would have to travel to London, try to make the wayward woman see sense, and, if he could not prevent the marriage, he

---

1 There are no records as to how George Howard first heard the news of Mary's impending nuptials, but he was certainly sent to London to 'sort her out'.

must at least ensure that Sir Richard Grenville would lay no claim to the Fitz estates, now in the hands of the Courtenays. Cutteford knew his place in the scheme of things, and agreed to travel to London; despite his natural misgivings about seeing Mary again, he was in no position to refuse. He promised to do all he could to arrange the matter to everyone's satisfaction, and in return, he announced – much to Richard Halse's surprise – that he had a few demands of his own.

Walreddon was first on his list. Not just as a place to live; George demanded the lease and all the income from the surrounding farms, and not just for his lifetime but for the lifetimes of both of his sons – for a period of ninety–nine years. George demanded that he be awarded the same status as the man he worked for. He felt that he and his family deserved to be landowners in their own right. Reluctantly, Halse agreed. The land was currently in the name of John Macy, who seems to have been a local official, and, after a legal battle between Cutteford and Macy[2], the estate was signed over to George and his family in 1629.[3]

And secondly – for there was more – George's eldest son wanted to study at the Middle Temple and train to be a lawyer, just like Richard Halse. Now George was a landowner, his son would be permitted to enter the Inns of Court, and the Middle Temple seemed a good place to start. Richard Halse, who trained at the Inner Temple, did not refuse the request, and George arranged for two guarantors for his son's entry to the Middle Temple in 1628.[4] His guarantors would both

---

2   See document C 2/ChasI/C32/71, held at the National Archives, London.

3   See document D1508/Moger/436, held at Devon Record Office, which notes the original document of conveyance to George Cutteford of 1627/1628.

4   See archives of the Middle Temple: George Cutteford's entry was kindly confirmed by Hannah Baker, their archivist, quoting: '29 November 1628 Mr George, son and heir-apparent of George Cutteford of Tavestoke, Devon, esq., specially; bound with William Tothill and John Maynard, esqs; fine, 4l.' William Tothill was an attorney in Exeter whose only son and heir had died; he subsequently became a philanthropist. John Maynard is likely to have been the man who would become Sir John Maynard, serjeant-at-law.

be wealthy attorneys and themselves graduates of the Middle Temple: William Tothill from Exeter and their old family friend, John Maynard. George Cutteford's eldest son achieved the professional and social status that George himself had never been able to afford. William Cutteford the sailor would have been delighted and astonished by their success.

Now there was only Sir Richard Grenville to contend with, and George travelled to London to meet with the prospective groom. The two men, of such differing backgrounds, hated each other at first sight.

The Grenville family were among the largest landowners in Cornwall; the family home, called Stowe, was once located a few miles west of the village of Kilkhampton on the northern coast of Cornwall. Nothing remains of Stowe manor but a few stables that are now part of a farm above Coombe valley, a rather bleak but picturesque basin that leads down to the sandy beach at Duckpool.

The Grenvilles had a long history of loyal service to the monarchy, as admirals and soldiers, MPs and Sheriffs, many sacrificing their lives in battle. Sir Roger Grenville drowned when he was captain of the *Mary Rose* as the ship was disastrously sunk in Portsmouth, during Henry VIII's battle against invading French forces.[5] In 1591, an elder Sir Richard Grenville died on the *Revenge* under attack from the Spanish Armada, heroically choosing to go down fighting with his ship rather than flee with the rest of the English fleet. The elder Sir Richard Grenville left two sons, the younger John battling to secure the Grenville's lands in Ireland against the riots of the Munster uprisings. The elder son, Bernard, was not regarded as a fighting man, though he was knighted for his services in Ireland. Bernard Grenville was generally content to live a quieter life, managing the family's many estates, including those of his wealthy wife.

Sir Bernard Grenville had four sons and two daughters. The family are immortalised by Daphne Du Maurier in her

---

5   Sansom, 2010, gives an excellent account of the sinking of the *Mary Rose*.

book *The King's General of the West.*[6] She describes Richard
Grenville, one of Bernard's younger sons, as a taciturn fighting man, fierce in his loyalties and often brutal in his actions.
This reflects Richard's character in later life, but at the time
he met Lady Mary Howard, Richard was considered to be
an attractive man of wit and humour, a flamboyant success
in the colourful court of King Charles I; a man who was
brave in battle, enjoyed carousing with beautiful women and
drinking heavily with his good friend and mentor, the Duke
of Buckingham. He was also a man of some intelligence,
studying at Exeter College in Oxford, and later in life studying mathematics at Leiden[7], though he never seems to have
completed any of his studies, preferring a life of action to
a life of intellectual endeavour. His enemies would declare
he was a 'notable whoremaster'[8], others would call him the
'red fox'[9] on account of his ruthless actions and his long red
hair, symbolic of virility and courage in the early seventeenth
century. But these insults just added to his lusty reputation
and his appeal.

Born in June 1600, so four years younger than Mary Howard,
Richard was the second son of Sir Bernard Grenville and he was
brought up on stories of his heroic ancestors. Like his grandfather and namesake, Richard was determined to be a hero. He
had all the right attributes: looks, courage, wit and intelligence.
All he lacked was the money to fund his preferred lifestyle.

His elder brother Bevil, though no coward, was more
like their father, staid and serious, an upstanding member of
Cornish society, more than able to take on the responsibilities of his inheritance. Richard was the exact opposite. He was
profligate in his spending and known to have a fiery temper,
arguing constantly with his older brother over loans and mort-
gages, papers and legal matters that bored Richard to death.

6   Du Maurier, 1946.

7   Miller, 1979.

8   Miller, 1979.

9   Miller, 1979.

While Bevil was admired, Richard was popular, especially with the soldiers he led into battle.

By 1628, Richard was a veteran of war. As the younger son, he had little to inherit from his father[10], and was expected to make his own way in the world. Like many a younger son before him, he chose fighting as a career, at just eighteen, fighting with the English forces in Holland against Spain. He then joined Sir Horace Vere's regiment defending the lands of King James I's son-in-law, Frederick V, in his battle for Bohemia that would become the Thirty Years War.[11] These were brutal wars, renowned for the slaughter of civilians. The English regiment under Vere, like many of the time, were unpaid, so were often forced to support themselves by plunder and looting the local populations – desperate behaviour that would shape the future battles in Ireland and the English Civil War.

As they defended Heidelberg, Frankenthal and Mannheim against the Hapsburg Emperor, Sir Richard fought alongside many English soldiers who would later gain prominence in the English Civil War: Royalists like Sir Ralph Hopton and George Goring, and Parliamentary supporters such as the Earls of Essex and Warwick, Thomas Fairfax, Philip Skippon and Sir William Waller. Though outnumbered and forced to surrender, after battling for a long five years Grenville earned a reputation as a gallant officer and a fearless fighter, and rose to the rank of Captain.

During a subsequent attack on Cadiz, led by King Charles I's favourite, the Duke of Buckingham, Grenville learned many valuable lessons about army discipline. Grenville's battles alongside the Duke so shaped his character, and informed his future actions, that it is worth describing the attack on Cadiz, and the reasons for the attack, in more detail.

During the last years of his life, King James I sent his son Charles and the Duke of Buckingham to Spain to arrange a

10 Miller, 1979, mentions properties Grenville inherited from his mother.
11 Miller, 1979, gives an excellent, detailed account of Grenville's involvement in the Thirty Years War.

marriage between Charles and the Spanish Infanta, Maria Anna of Spain, a devout Catholic. James saw this alliance as a means of achieving peace in Europe, which was then embroiled in the Catholic versus Protestant battles of the Thirty Years War.

The marriage negotiations failed, leaving Charles and his friend Buckingham thoroughly humiliated. In retaliation, Buckingham called for a declaration of war against Spain, and in the early years of Charles's reign, Buckingham despatched a naval attack on Cadiz, under the command of Lord Wimbledon. Richard Grenville took command of a company of infantry in the regiment of Sir John Burgh, a commander admired for his discipline.[12]

Supplies for the expedition were generally poor, with the food rotten; many men died of food poisoning and exposure due to the lack of adequate clothing. Soon after landing on the Spanish coast, the English army went in search of a Spanish force thought to be close at hand. The officers under Lord Wimbledon forgot to bring ashore food for the men, so after miles of walking, the men were exhausted and thirsty. Seeing they had no supplies, Lord Wimbledon instructed them to raid the local houses for casks of wine. The result was mayhem – the drunken soldiers, with empty stomachs, raided the entire village, fighting between themselves over barrels of wine and any food they could find. The invasion went no further, and the English returned home in disordered disgrace.

Richard Grenville was not among the drunken forces, staying with his own regiment on the outskirts of Cadiz, but the disorderly conduct of Wimbledon's soldiers taught Grenville the value of discipline, and the need for reliable supplies for the fighting men. He would ensure both during the English Civil War, at a terrible cost to the local population.

In 1627, even after Charles's marriage to a French princess, Henrietta Maria, war broke out between England and France. Buckingham was sent to lead forces to capture the island of

---

12 Miller, 1979, p. 11.

Rhe, to protect the Huguenot city of La Rochelle on France's west coast. Grenville was commissioned as Major in charge of one of the regiments, and was knighted by Buckingham just prior to the expedition.

Again supplies were short, and discipline poor. When the French attacked, only the discipline of Sir John Burgh and his regiment prevented complete disaster, and casualties were high, including the loss of Sir John himself. Grenville was wounded (though not seriously).

After three and a half months of fierce fighting, the English forces retreated. Hundreds drowned or were slaughtered by the French in the retreat, leaving La Rochelle and the Huguenots at the mercy of the French. Buckingham was forced to shoulder the blame for the failure of the expedition, with 3,000 men killed – half the expeditionary force.

Buckingham tried again to relieve La Rochelle, but Grenville – literally – missed the boat. Sir Richard was not on board his ship when the fleet sailed from Portsmouth. He frantically rode to Plymouth in an attempt to meet the fleet there, but the ships were faster than his horse, and again they set sail before he could embark, leaving Sir Richard to write an embarrassing letter of apology to the Secretary of State.[13] It was not the last time his decadent lifestyle would interfere with his duties.

Between his military duties, Sir Richard Grenville represented Fowey in the House of Commons, and was probably in London in 1628 on Parliamentary business when the Duke of Buckingham brought to his attention the arrival of a widow called Lady Mary Howard, whose attractions were greatly increased by the size of her estates.

Sir Richard, then twenty-eight, was having problems with money. A soldier's life was poorly paid, with most income coming from pillage, and once home, he needed money to live the fine life to which he aspired. Richard found himself

13 Miller, 1979, p. 16.

in constant arguments with his older and rather pious brother over some land Richard was trying to mortgage, and Richard quickly became exasperated.

Richard now owed money to many creditors, including Sir Henry Spry's family, though Sir Henry had died soon after his return from the disaster at the island of Rhe. More ominously, Richard also owed substantial sums to Sir William Courtenay. A wealthy heiress was just what he needed, though marriage to Sir William's granddaughter proved to be the worse decision he could have made.

Mary was still engaged in a court battle against Sir Theophilus Howard, now the Earl of Suffolk after his father's death in 1626. Richard was only too happy to ingratiate himself into her cause. A widow's jointure of £600 a year was worth the effort, with the prospect of so much more to come if they married. The defendant, Theophilus Howard, was, after all, the son of the man responsible for the death of Grenville's heroic grandfather, killed on the *Revenge*. There was no love lost between Theophilus Howard and Richard Grenville.

Mary was excited by the attentions of this younger, gallant officer. As a widow, she was at last able to choose her own husband, and Richard was quite a prize. So what if her grandfather and the Courtenays did not approve? So what if they thought Richard was only after the income from her estates? She was convinced of Grenville's affections and of her own heart – and King Charles himself thought that a match between two powerful families of the south west counties was a wonderful idea.

The existing portrait of Sir Richard was probably painted sometime in 1628 by Cavaliero Moro[14], when Sir Richard was twenty-eight. Richard is depicted in his armour, with a cravat of lace at his neck, a not uncommon affectation at the time.

---

14 It is difficult to identify exactly which artist painted Sir Richard Grenville's portrait. Certainly he was called Cavaliero Moro, but there were a number of artists of the surname Moro in Europe. It is likely Sir Richard, along with many fighting in Europe at the time, had his portrait painted at the studios on one such Moro.

There is something of a soft fleshiness about his face, very like his older brother Bevil, and a very sensual mouth that, to the modern viewer, is quite feminine. Sadly the reproductions are so poor that we lose the style of his famous hair, but the overall effect reveals Sir Richard to have been an attractive suitor.

With hindsight, there is also an aspect of his expression that is disturbing, a hint of the violent passions resting beneath the surface. He was a passionate man, flamboyant and witty in court, but also as fiery in battle, with a disturbing taste for brutality and death.

The marriage between Mary Howard and Sir Richard Grenville would prove to be as passionate and volatile as the two individuals themselves.

Still partying in London, Mary must have been shocked to discover George Cutteford at her door; he had travelled all the way from Tavistock to see her. Perhaps, she thought, he was jealous and had come to persuade her not to marry Sir Richard, or come to wish her well. Or, as it turned out, he could be there on behalf of her grandfather to ensure that Richard Grenville gained no access to the Fitz fortunes. Needless to say, they argued about the impending marriage, the determined Mary refusing to sway from her amorous intentions. Having failed to prevent the marriage, George Cutteford changed his tactics, and offered Mary an alternative – he had papers drawn up that conveyed the Fitz estates, or at least Mary's interest in them, to three trustees from Tavistock. This gave Sir Richard Grenville no claim on the estate, and no access to any of its income without Mary's explicit approval. It was an unusual 'pre-nuptial agreement' that would satisfy Sir William Courtenay.

Mary appears to have been happy to agree to the deal. It left her in control of the income from the Fitz estates, and she had the power to permit her new husband to benefit from that income if she wanted. Now they just had to convince Sir Richard to sign it. How they managed this is unknown. Certainly he did not understand the implications of the contract.

It must have been a dark day for George Cutteford, presenting the final document to Richard Grenville to sign, surrounded by witnesses. George's old friend, John Maynard, was there, and George Radford, probably Cutteford's son-in-law. The men all knew they were conspiring to deceive Sir Richard Grenville, and deny him access to the Fitz estates. It was a day they would all come to regret. If there was a moment when George Cutteford damned himself, this was it.

Later, Sir Richard would declare in court that he had signed without reading the document, and he was probably telling the truth. Mary, meanwhile, would see his signature as proof that he was marrying her for love not money. They were married in November 1628[15], and Sir Richard soon acquainted himself with all of his wife's possessions and saw that as much money as possible was squeezed out of the tenants.

Some say it was Mary herself who had the contract drawn up by Cutteford, distrusting her husband enough to want to protect her interests. Having helped her with her successful claim against Sir Theophilus Howard, it seems strange that Mary would initiate such proceedings against Sir Richard just before they were married. She did not have to marry Sir Richard; as a widow, she was enjoying an independent life, and it seems odd that she would choose to marry a man she did not trust. Sir Richard arrived in Devon happily assuming his role as the wealthy Lord of the Manor, but oblivious to the true nature of his new-found status.

The marriage would become a disaster for everyone concerned.

---

15 Radford, 1890, p. 80. There is some uncertainty of the exact date of their marriage, some quoting October, others December, but they were certainly married in the autumn of 1628.

Chapter Six

A Marriage Under Fire

In May 1630, Mary gave birth to a son, baptised Richard Grenville, in the church at Tavistock.[1] The baptism ceremony must have been quite a spectacle. Edward Courtenay, the youngest son of Sir William Courtenay, attended the church to represent Mary's cousins, and to explain, in no uncertain terms, to Sir Richard that his newborn son could never have any claim to the Fitz estates.

Lulworth Castle, home of Theophilus Howard.

---

1   Radford, 1890, p. 81.

Sir Richard of course flew into a rage at the news; he attacked Edward and they fought. In the midst of the brawl, Sir Richard and Edward Courtenay were dragged away by officers of the law, and imprisoned in the Gatehouse in London, subject to a formal investigation by the King's Privy Council.[2] The arrest was ironic, considering Sir Richard had been recently appointed a justice of the peace.

George Cutteford appears not to have been involved in the debacle. He was, during 1630, working as an attorney for the Court of the Stannaries, probably pleased to have found regular employment away from the intrigues of the Fitz estates. It was possible though that Sir Francis Courtenay, as the new Lord Warden of the Stannaries, had offered George Cutteford the position.[3] It would not be long before George was drawn back into the battles at Fitzford – and into a furious assault on his own life.

Sir William Courtenay, then seventy-seven years old, journeyed to London to support his son Edward at the hearing, but the trial became too much for the old man, and Sir William died in June 1630. Strangely, the co-trustee of the Fitz estates, William Herbert, 3rd Earl of Pembroke, died the same year, aged just fifty years old. The Pembroke title passed to William Herbert's brother, Phillip, who was a friend and ally of Richard Grenville. Suddenly ownership of the Fitz estates was within Grenville's reach.

The investigation into the battle between Sir Richard and Edward Courtenay was then delayed while Edward and his

---

2 See L1508M/E/Legal/Court and Estate papers/39 for further details of the arrest, held at Devon Record Office. Miller, 1979, incorrectly identifies Edward Courtenay as a servant of the Howards.

3 George Cutteford received payments from the Stannary Court during 1630. After the death of the 3rd Earl of Pembroke in 1630, who was then the Lord Warden of the Stannaries, it seems the Warden title was transferred directly to his brother, Philip Herbert, the 4th Earl of Pembroke, but there was a delay. Some records show the title passing first to Francis Courtenay. It's possible that Francis Courtenay inherited the title of Deputy Lord Warden of the Stannaries, from his father, and acted as the Lord Warden for a period just after the death of the 3rd Earl of Pembroke.

family arranged for Sir William's body to be transported back to Powderham Castle. Sir Richard was forced to languish for months in the horrific cells of the Gatehouse prison, under the orders of his arch-enemy Sir Theophilus Howard, a senior figure in the Privy Council.[4] Edward was released from the Gatehouse, by the same Privy Council, probably in June 1630, to attend his father's funeral, but returned to London for the hearing.

Sir Richard Grenville then tried to have Edward Courtenay murdered. Edward petitioned the Privy Council to complain that Sir Richard, still incarcerated, had hired men to have him killed.

In November 1630, as Edward described in detail, he was heading home to his lodgings, passing between the two gates at Whitehall, when half a dozen men attacked him; one of them he recognised as a kinsman of Sir Richard Grenville. Edward was sure they had meant to murder him, though he seems to have valiantly fought them off. He accused Sir Richard of attempted murder, and two of the assassins admitted to Lord Sheriff Fulford that Sir Richard had hired them to that purpose. The Privy Council, which included the Earl of Dorset[5], issued yet another warrant for the arrest of Sir Richard Grenville.

This is the earliest evidence that Sir Richard was prepared to hire thugs to commit murder on his behalf, an ominous warning of his future actions. Sir Richard was not released until 23 December 1630[6], having spent seven long months in gaol.

While Sir Richard remained locked up in London, Mary appears to have taken her own revenge against the Courtenays. It is not known how, but suddenly the Court of

---

4   See L1508M/E/Court and Estate papers/39 for Theophilus Howard's signature as a member of the Privy Council.

5   See L1508M/E/Court and Estate papers/39 for the Earl of Dorset's signature as a member of the Privy Council.

6   Penfold, P.A., 1964, as reproduced on British History Online: www.british-history.ac.uk.

Wards were made aware of the existence of her son George Halse, now eight years old and living still with Ann Halse, probably at Kenedon.

George Halse was declared to be the son of the late Sir Charles Howard and therefore the true heir to the Fitz estates. However, as a minor he came under the protection of the Court of Wards – who could now, as they had done with his mother, auction him off to a new guardian. As was usual practice, the boy was taken away from his adopted family at Kenedon, and into care in London while the matter was addressed and a guardian appointed.

The Courtenays must have been horrified. Sir William was dead; young Edward's life was being threatened by Sir Richard Grenville, and now they were faced with the prospect of losing the Fitz estates to the Howard family. The Howards themselves were ignorant of the boy's existence, and certainly were surprised to discover Sir Charles had had a son.

Robert Howard, a younger brother of Theophilus, had inherited Clun Castle in Shropshire after the death of his elder brother Charles and was shocked when, in 1631, the Court of Wards sued him for the return of the Clun estates – which they said now belonged to some previously unknown nephew.[7]

The Howards knew that George Halse was illegitimate; Sir Charles had been out of the country for eighteen months before the boy was born. Robert Howard tried to reclaim the Clun Estates, on the grounds of George Halse's illegitimacy, but, as Robert did not know who the child's real father was, the Court of Wards would hear none of it. Robert must have been furious, as of course he himself had been prosecuted and imprisoned by Sir Edmund Coke for adultery with Sir Edmund's daughter Frances, yielding an illegitimate child. Now, here was his sister-in-law's illegitimate son taking Robert's inheritance away from him![8]

---

7   Miller, 1979, p. 180n.
8   Miller, 1979, p. 180n.

How did the Court of Wards discover George Halse? There are a number of possible scenarios. Perhaps Mary or George, resentful of the interference of the Halses, finally decided they wanted their son back with them after so many years apart. Perhaps George Cutteford accidentally informed his friend the Earl of Dorset that he had a son called George Halse. Dorset and his cousins the Howards were still struggling financially, and Halse's claim to the Fitz estates was a welcome opportunity, as it could be argued that George Halse was in fact Charles Howard's son. It was to everyone's benefit to keep Richard Grenville away from the Fitz fortunes, and an heir to Charles Howard was an unexpected solution. Perhaps Sir Richard had discovered there was another son and, in an attack on the Courtenays, announced the boy's existence to the Privy Council – though this might have disinherited his own child, so it seems unlikely. There is no evidence to prove the events and motivations that led up to the 'outing' of George Halse. But George Cutteford quite brilliantly manipulated the events to his own benefit.

The Court of Wards seemed not to have questioned why the boy was hidden away, though the fact that his new step-father was in the Gatehouse for maliciously injuring the boy's relatives gave them a good idea of the circumstances. George Halse obviously needed the protection of a fine, upstanding – and preferably wealthy – citizen, to remove him from the violence of the Grenvilles and the scheming Courtenays.

The Court of Wards saw saving George Halse as its duty, and George Cutteford helpfully had just the guardian in mind. Cutteford himself could not afford to buy the boy and Mary's finances were either entailed away or suffering from outstanding debts. However, there was a rich man he could trust to take care of his son (for a large fee) – the man was called Sir Francis Trelawney.

Historians describe the life of George Halse as tragic[9]; taken from his parents at birth to live with distant relatives; purchased

---

9   Miller, 1979, pp. 22 and 23.

at eight via the Court of Wards and placed into the care of a complete stranger. But George Halse's life was not so tragic, for Sir Francis Trelawney was no stranger. Trelawney was related to a very successful Plymouth merchant and Cornish landowners, many of the family rich and powerful, some MPs in Plymouth, all linked by marriage to the families of Sir Francis Drake and Sir John Hawkins[10], wealthy and notorious men.

Francis Trelawney was a respected justice of the peace, and an affluent man, and married into the Seymour family (whose influence over the court of Henry VIII had brought them great renown).[11] Trelawney's purse was vast; he was known to loan thousands of pounds to his relatives[12]; and his charity appeared endless. All in all, he was a good man and a good friend to George Cutteford. Where the money came from is unclear; a loan here, another there. George probably mortgaged Walreddon itself to raise the huge sums involved.

Of course, it helped that Sir Francis Trelawney was also the brother-in-law of Sir Francis Courtenay. Their wives were sisters, both daughters of Edward Seymour.[13] The arrangements were made with Sir Francis Trelawney, who knew full well that the boy was the illegitimate son of George Cutteford. Most people in the Tavistock area would have known the truth, and yet nothing was said; nothing was mentioned to Sir Richard

---

10 Sir John Hawkins' mother was Joan Trelawney; see http://en.wikipedia.org/wiki/John_Hawkins. There are many excellent biographies and genealogical charts online, which show the extent of the intermarriages between the Trelawneys, the Hawkins family, the Courteneys, the Drakes and the Seymours in Devon in the seventeenth century.

11 Records indicate that Margaret Seymour, the daughter of Edward Seymour of Berry Pomeroy, 2nd Baronet, married Francis Trelawney, son of the High Sheriff of Cornwall, John Trelawney. This is likely to be the Francis Trelawney described in Miller, 1979, guardian to George Halse. See http://en.wikipedia.org/wiki/Sir_Edward_Seymour,_2nd_Baronet. Edward Seymour's grandfather was the elder brother of Jane Seymour, third wife of King Henry VIII.

12 Letters from Edward Seymour, 3rd Baronet, indicate that his brother-in-law, Francis Trelawney, loaned his son, Ned Seymour, £1,300, which took some time to pay back.

13 Elizabeth Seymour married Sir Francis Courtenay; her younger sister Margaret married Francis Trelawney.

when he did eventually come home. The people of Tavistock
appear to have kept the secret quite safe, and supported George
Cutteford in his plans for his son.

Previously it was thought that George Halse was sent off to
some stranger[14], but that was the genius of George Cutteford's
solution. His son became hidden in plain sight. For the plan
was not to sell his son off to just some other guardian – the
plan was to bring his son home.

You have only to look at a map of the area around Tavistock
to realise the beauty of the new arrangements. Sir Francis's
main residence at the time was Venn House, located in the
small village of Lamerton, just north-west of Tavistock. His
fine estate bordered the Fitz estate, while Walreddon was just
a little further south across the river Tavy; neither more than
half an hour's ride away from Trelawney's estate. George Halse
moved in next door. He would never live far away from his
mother again for the rest of his life. George Cutteford, with
Mary's help, had played the Court of Wards at its own game,
and brought his son to his own door.

Fortunately, it seems the arrangements for George Halse's
guardianship were finalised before Sir Richard was released
from the Gatehouse prison, leaving Sir Richard unaware that
the heir to the Fitz estates was living just next door. Finally
released in December 1630, Sir Richard returned to Fitzford
embittered by the Courtenays' treatment of him, raging against
his persecutors, the Earls of Suffolk and Dorset on the Privy
Council. Sadly for Mary, he took out his terrifying rage on her.

Their marriage had never been free from problems. In
November 1629, Grenville had begun a series of lawsuits,
trying to relieve them of Mary's outstanding debts to the
Court of Wards.[15] Mary's chief creditor was George Cutteford
and Sir Richard was determined to prove that George had
obtained the lease to the Walreddon estates by dishonest means.

---

14 Miller, 1979, p. 72.

15 Miller, 1979, p. 186n, gives an excellent and detailed explanation for Mary's
    outstanding debts to the Court of Wards.

The old gatehouse at Tavistock, all that remains of the Fitzford estate, though the gatehouse was in fact rebuilt in the nineteenthth century and moved slightly from its original location. (Photograph by Dr Tom Greeves, MA, PhD, www.tomgreeves.org)

Left: Front cover of *The Bloodie Book of John Fitz*, originally published in the seventeenth century, and thought to have been written by the Earl of Northumberland's chaplain, who witnessed the events. This image is from Sabine Baring-Gould's *Devonshire Characters and Strange Events* published in 1908.

Present-day New Street in Plymouth, 'new' in the late 1500s, and location of the Elizabethan House. Throughout the seventeenth century, small row houses like these would have housed up to six sailors and their families. (Photograph by Penny Mayes, 2005, www.geograph.org.uk)

A view of Sutton Pool Harbour in Plymouth today. The area is known as the Barbican, referring to the old castle that used to protect the port. The castle had four towers and was known as the Castle Quadrant. When the castle fell into ruins by the mid-seventeenth century, the stones were used to build the Royal Citadel near Plymouth Hoe. (Photograph by James Cridland, www.jamescridland.net)

A seventeenth-century painting of English ships of the Royal Navy. Sadly, the artist remains unidentified. (Image reproduced with the kind permission of the Duesseldorfer Auktionshaus, www.duesseldorfer-auktionshaus.planetactive.com)

The Fitz memorial in the parish church at Tavistock, with the images of the parents of John Fitz lying with a lion and a lamb at their feet. (Photograph by Dr Tom Greeves MA PhD, www.tomgreeves.org)

Tavistock today, showing the view down West Street, the parish church of St Eustachius on the right, with the moors ahead. (West Devon District Council, from Tavistock Tourist Information, 2011)

The picturesqe ruins of Okehampton. (Library of Congress, Prints & Photographs Division, LC-DIG-ppmsc-08759)

Powderham Castle on the River Exe, ancestral home to the Courtenay family, and now ancestral home to the Earl of Devon, reproduced with kind permission of Lord Devon. (Photograph by Rinus Kool)

Victorian Tavistock. (Library of Congress, Prints & Photographs Division LC-DIG-ppmsc-08890)

Right: St Eustachius' parish church in the heart of Tavistock. (Photograph reproduced with the kind permission of Tavistock Tourist Information)

Audley End, Saffron Walden, the palatial estate of the Howard family in the seventeenth century. (Photograph by Steve McShane, www.geograph.org.uk)

Clun Castle in Shropshire (Photograph by Philip Halling, 2006, www.geograph.org.uk)

The ominous remains of Lydford Castle, located near Lydford, to the west of the road between Tavistock and Okehampton. (Photograph by Dr Tom Greeves, MA, PhD, www.tomgreeves.org)

West Down near Walreddon. The image is taken from Buckland, facing West Down, with the Walkham River in the valley below, flowing to the left (the west) to join the Tavy at Double Water. Walreddon Manor is located over the hill to the left. The cottage in the picture is Buckator, once owned by the tin mines. (Photograph by Dr Tom Greeves, MA, PhD, www.tomgreeves.org)

Lady Mary Howard
(1596-1671), an
etching by Hollar
done in 1657, after the
painting by van Dyke
finished sometime
around 1628.
Reproduced from
Sabine Baring-Gould's
*Devonshire Characters
and Strange Events*.

Sir Richard Grenville
(1600-1659), a painting
by Caveliero Moro
completed sometime
in 1626-1628 and
reproduced from
Richard Granville's
*The History of the
Granville Family*,
published in 1895.

Having someone like Cutteford as a neighbour must have been galling to a man like Sir Richard, proud of his own heroic status and heritage. Cutteford was the son of a humble sailor; a mere attorney with a Puritan background, educated in charitable schools and never reaching university. Sir Richard does not seem to have suspected that George Cutteford was his wife's former lover – he was just the steward, after all.

However, Sir Richard was suspicious of George and Mary's friendship and, on his return from the Gatehouse prison, believed that they had conspired together to mislead him into signing the agreement, which left him and his newborn son without income or status. He was right to be suspicious – he certainly had grounds to be paranoid – but his behaviour did nothing to support his cause.

In 1631, Sir Richard broke into Walreddon and stole away Cutteford's documents pertaining to Mary's finances, probably including the agreement and Cutteford's claim to Walreddon. Reading the small print – and these documents were ludicrously complicated – Sir Richard finally realised how precarious was his own financial situation, and how guile and lies had caught him.

When George Cutteford met with Grenville to request the return of his papers, Sir Richard threatened George's life, probably at sword-point, and George was forced to retreat for his own safety.[16]

Mary would face the consequences of Sir Richard's anger alone, but Sir Richard would be surprised by the strength of her reactions. She resented Sir Richard's behaviour towards Cutteford and was outraged at Richard's conduct. In papers later presented to the Court of High Commission during her request for a separation it was reported that he called his wife a whore, publicly denouncing her as such before justices of the peace. Of all the insults to a woman of the time, 'whore' was the worst.[17]

---

16 Miller, 1979, p. 28.
17 Gowing, 1996.

Richard imprisoned Mary in a small corner of Fitzford, refusing her any say over the running of the house or the estate, and instead putting his aunt, Catherine Abbott, in charge of the household, while he claimed all the rent from the tenants for himself. Mary was forced to appeal to the courts for money for her living expenses.

When Mary refused to speak to Richard, he tried to suffocate her; he ordered the servants to burn horse hair, wool, feathers and the parings from horses' hooves, forcing the smoke into her chambers through a hole in the kitchen wall. On another occasion, Sir Richard broke down her door, sword in hand, and threatened her life. Subsequently, Mary became pregnant; their second child, Elizabeth, was born sometime around October 1631, though there is no record of her baptism.[18] Richard refused Mary a midwife of her own choosing, despite her protestations, and the entire affair suggests that he forced himself upon her. Mary would never be much of a mother to Elizabeth, having no regard for the child and refusing to see her even in later life; this suggests that Mary was still haunted by the violence surrounding her conception.

While Mary was pregnant, she stole the key from Sir Richard's closet[19] and when she refused to return it, he grabbed her petticoat, gave her a black eye and threw her to the ground. In his defence, Sir Richard declared to the court that she had locked him in his closet, and, after breaking free, he had hit her in retaliation. She had, he said, called him terrible names: 'an unseemly fellow' and 'a poor rogue'[20]; and would sing lewd songs to provoke him, proclaiming he was not worth ten groats when he married her, and shouting that she had good friends in London who would come to her aid. On his leaving once for business, she had wished that 'the devil and sixpence go with him, and so he shall lack neither money nor company.'[21]

18   Radford, 1890.

19   Radford, 1890, p. 82.

20   Radford, 1890, p. 82.

21   Miller, 1979, p. 32.

Sir Richard advised the court that he suspected his wife was committing adultery, as she would travel away from home without servants, having told him that she loved other men better than him – including, heaven forbid, George Cutteford. In fact, she was probably travelling secretly to visit her son, George Halse, living at that time with Sir Francis Trelawney just up the road in Lamerton. It is doubtful she was continuing her relationship with George Cutteford, who was reconciled with his family at Walreddon.

Her good friends in London did come to her aid. While Grenville was busy suing the Earl of Suffolk, Theophilus Howard, for payment of the widow's jointure owing to Mary, Mary in turn became friends again with the Howard family, who gladly supported her case for a separation from Sir Richard. The Howard-Grenville feud raged on.

By the autumn of 1631, Mary was in fear for her life. George Cutteford probably helped her to get word of her situation to Theophilus Howard, who then initiated her request for a separation from Richard. The Howards sent a servant called Francis Taylor to escort Mary from Fitzford to London for the hearing.

Mary was pregnant with Sir Richard's child Elizabeth at the time. It is uncertain where Elizabeth was born, as there is no mention of her birth in the Tavistock records. The child could not have been born before September 1631, so it is possible Mary was already in London, but the court proceedings describe Mary and Richard having terrible arguments over the choice of midwife for the birth. Soon after, the baby Elizabeth is mentioned as a resident at Fitzford. The most feasible scenario is that Mary gave birth to Elizabeth at Fitzford. Her post-child-birth 'veiling' must have hidden a few bruises. Theophilus Howard's servant then arrived at the house, probably aided by George Cutteford, and with a warrant to have Mary removed. They may have had to wait until Mary was fit to travel.

On receiving the warrant, Grenville flew into a rage – but in the chaos they managed to get the veiled Mary to a horse and away. She would have said a hurried goodbye to her new-born daughter and her little boy. It is most likely that, with roads so difficult, they took Mary to a boat, down the rivers to Plymouth harbour and, after bidding Cutteford farewell, she set sail for London.

So Mary found herself living with Theophilus Howard in London, having left her two young children at Fitzford in the care of Sir Richard Grenville's Aunt Catherine. Having fought so long for her claim to the Fitz estates, Mary must have found it galling to leave.

Meanwhile, George Halse, now nine years old, may have remained at Lamerton with his new guardian, though George Halse/Howard next appears in London some time later. It is possible Mary took him with her, with Cutteford smuggling the boy to Plymouth to travel with his mother. Her eldest daughter, Mary, whose father was Charles Howard, was then about seventeen and probably already married. She became Mary Vernon, already living in London. The Vernons were an old established family, who could trace their lineage back to the time of William the Conqueror. It is not certain which of the many Vernons Mary married, but she was at one time recorded as Mary Vernon of Islington, and there is a Vernon Square still in Islington, probably once the location of the Vernon's London residence. Mary Howard's eldest surviving daughter had married very well indeed.

Mary Howard's departure was far from the end of the matter. When the servant removed her from Fitzford, Sir Richard, in front of many witnesses, passionately denounced Theophilus Howard with the words, 'Tell him he is a base lord and hath used me basely, and he shall know as much'.[22] Theophilus Howard took the matter to the Star Chamber, who declared that Sir Richard's slander had 'touched the highest blood in the kingdom.'[23]

---

22 Miller, 1979, p. 34.
23 Miller, 1979, p. 35.

On 3 February 1632, the Star Chamber fined Sir Richard £8,000 for his insults: £4,000 to be paid to the King, the rest to Theophilus Howard. Grenville was incarcerated in the Fleet Prison in London. The Star Chamber was legendary for its severe penalties for seditious libel against ministers of the Crown. As well as being a member of the King's Privy Council, Theophilus Howard was the Lord Warden of the Cinque Ports[24], having been appointed to the post after the assassination of the Duke of Buckingham. The Star Chamber was not impressed by slander against one of their own.

Even so, the penalty against Sir Richard was considered unusually harsh, even for the Chamber. Just six days later, the Court of High Commission considered Mary's petition for a separation, and demanded Grenville also pay his wife alimony of £350 a year.

Of course, Sir Richard couldn't pay the fine or the alimony. He no longer had any access to the income from Mary's estates. New trustees had been appointed: Philip Herbert, who had inherited his brother's title as the new Earl of Pembroke; and George Cutteford's old friend the Earl of Dorset.[25] The odds against Sir Richard claiming any income were stacking up fast. His disastrous marriage was ruining his life.

Meanwhile, the tenants of the Fitz estates were protesting that they would not pay their rents, as they no longer knew to whom it was due. Not surprising considering the number of trustees, owners and leaseholders who had claimed the Fitz estates over the years: John Fitz, the Courtenays, all of Mary's husbands and on to the Earls of Pembroke and Dorset, all in the space of less than thirty years. The tenants couldn't keep up with all the changes in management.

In Fleet prison, Sir Richard was in a sorry state. Prisoners were dependent for their upkeep on the support of friends and relatives, but Sir Richard had no one left willing to assist him.

---

24 For a list of the Lord Wardens of the Cinque Ports, see: http://en.wikipedia.org/wiki/Lord_Warden_of_the_Cinque_Ports#17th_century

25 Radford, 1890.

He had been taken from his luxurious life at Fitzford and ended up starving in the filthy conditions at the Fleet, unable to satisfy any of his many creditors.

While he was in prison, one of his servants at Fitzford was accused of stealing Grenville's clothes. The items included a fine linen shirt embroidered with gold and pearls, a waistcoat worked with silver gilt and gems, and 100 linen cuffs valued then at over £100.[26] Grenville was obviously a man of extravagant tastes, now reduced to severe deprivation.

To make matters worse for Sir Richard, Sir Francis Courtenay stepped up his own attacks on the poor man. Two of Sir Francis' officials turned up at Fitzford to search for evidence of coin clipping, a terrible crime in the seventeenth century where valuable metals were clipped from the edges of coins to be smelted and sold; the equivalent of theft from the Crown.[27] As an official of the Stannaries, it was Sir Francis Courtenay's duty to have the matter investigated.

It seems that Sir Richard's household had been warned they were coming. Although the officials interrogated the servants, including Sir Richard's Aunt Catherine, and pulled the house apart in search of tools and other evidence, what little they found was insufficient to support a prosecution.

Meanwhile, the children left at Fitzford were suffering in much-reduced circumstances. Mary was battling with Sir Richard to be given permission to see them, while Sir Richard refused her access to their children until he was discharged of all her debts, for which, as her husband, he remained liable – despite their separation. Mary Howard countered that she would pay him nothing until she was permitted to see her children. The battle raged on and on.

Sir Richard made a desperate appeal to the Earl of Dorset, to require Mary to provide for the needs of their children, for his own needs while in prison, and for his aunt still overseeing the

---

26 Miller, 1979, p. 28.

27 Miller, 1979, p. 33.

household at Fitzford. It appears that Mary grudgingly obliged, and at the same time obtained a 'divorce'[28] from Sir Richard, on grounds of his having had an adulterous relationship during their marriage, one that had resulted in an illegitimate child. An ironic claim, considering her own extra-marital affairs; there is no information on the identity of the bastard child or the other woman involved. In 1644, a young man called Joseph Grenville appeared during the English Civil War. Then sixteen, he was thought to be the illegitimate son of Sir Richard Grenville, and proof of Sir Richard's notorious womanising. Joseph must have been born sometime in 1628, just before (or soon after) Sir Richard married Mary, so perhaps Mary's case had some basis in fact.

Greater irony was yet to come. In December 1631, George Cutteford joined Sir Richard as an inmate of Fleet Prison.[29] Cutteford had been counter-sued by Grenville, for not paying Grenville the rent on the Walreddon Estate, and obstinately disobeying a Court Order to pay the arrears. Sir Richard must have been delighted to find his old adversary in the cell next door, but his pleasure was soon blighted. With assistance, probably from the Earl of Dorset, George was permitted by the Warden of Fleet Prison to come and go as he pleased and to live in his own lodgings without any restraint. George's close friendship with Theophilus Howard and the Earl of Dorset had paid off handsomely in George's favour, and George found himself staying at many fine homes in and around London for the period of his incarceration – the Howards and Mary were all in London, the Earl of Dorset was at nearby Knole House in Kent.

28 Miller, 1979, p. 38. Divorce was very expensive, and still very rare, in the seventeenth century, and certainly divorce did not exist in the modern sense, so Richard Grenville and Mary Howard were just formally separated by the courts. See Miller, 1979, p. 187n for a full explanation of the judicial processes involved. Although 'divorced', Sir Richard Grenville was still Mary Howard's husband by law and therefore still liable for her debts, even though he was also liable for alimony payments – a very inconvenient combination in his case. You have to feel a bit sorry for the poor man.

29 Miller, 1979, p. 187n.

It is quite probable that George re-established his relationship with Mary while they were there together.[30] In July 1631,
Mary re-affirmed in writing her lover's right to the Walreddon
Estates[31], so she and Cutteford were back on amicable terms,
almost as though her marriage to Sir Richard Grenville had
never happened.

It was not unusual for a prisoner to be allowed temporary
release to retrieve papers and sort out his affairs, but George's
situation was unusually relaxed. He might not have been in
prison at all, for all the luxurious lifestyle he 'suffered', and he
was eventually allowed to return home to Devon in June 1632,
leaving the furious Sir Richard to languish in prison for a further horrific sixteen months.[32]

In October 1633, Sir Richard managed to escape from
the Fleet prison, probably as a 'day release' who never
returned. He quickly found himself a fighting commission
with the Swedish army, still battling the Thirty Years War in
Germany. There Richard would remain for five years, bitterness brewing inside him, until at last he could exact his
revenge – not against the Courts or judges, the Howards,
or even his wife, though he had cause to despise them
all. No, his revenge was of a much more personal nature,
targeted specifically at 'that pious Puritan lawyer' and low-
status land-grabber, George Cutteford. George Cutteford
came to personify everything that Sir Richard despised
about the religious, economic and social changes occurring
in England. Cutteford, twenty years older than Richard,
probably reminded Richard of his elder brother and his
unyielding father. Cutteford was the prime target for all of
Richard's festering resentments.

---

30 Mary had houses at Southwark, on the banks of the Thames, and Lewisham,
   where George Cutteford likely stayed during his 'imprisonment'. The
   Howards also had residences in London, and the Earl of Dorset's fine estate of
   Knole was just south east of London.

31 D1508M/Moger/436, 1631. Held at Devon Record Office.

32 Miller, 1979, p. 38.

When Cutteford and Grenville met again, England would be in the thralls of Civil War, and Grenville would be awarded a free licence, by King Charles himself, to exact his own brand of sadistic revenge on anyone who had ever crossed him.

George Cutteford was first on his list.

PURITANS IN SEVENTEENTH CENTURY ENGLAND

The Puritans were an amorphous group rising from the English Protestant movement of the sixteenth and seventeenth century. Frequently used today as meaning the opposite of hedonism, with a preference for plain clothes and simple religious ceremonies, Puritanism was a term used at the time to refer to anyone who held particular or distinctive non-conformist views of religious rituals.

The Church of England had been officially formed under Queen Elizabeth I, but, for Puritan Protestants, the Church's rituals and hierarchies too much reflected Catholicism and popery. They hated the Book of Common Prayer introduced by King James I. They sought for purity of religious ritual, with nothing to separate the individual from their communications with God, hence their preference for simple decor in their meeting houses, and inspiring preachers rather than overbearing Latin-spouting bishops. Feeling persecuted by the Church of England, many congregations sought out more sympathetic communities, some heading off to Holland, and one such congregation making the famous voyage on the *Mayflower* to establish a colony in New England.[33]

---

33 Philbrick, 2006. A wonderful account not only of the journey of the *Mayflower,* but also the strange mix of people, both puritan and military, in that early settlement; Philbrick's depictions of puritan life, and its many contradictions, and their relationships with the native tribes of America, are superb.

Back at home, under Charles I and his Archbishop Laud, and influenced by Catholic Queen Henrietta Maria, the Church of England grew even more Catholic in nature, with Church decoration taking on a grand scale and the congregation separated from the altar and the rituals of mass by newly-installed railings. This was not the personal relationship with God to which the Puritans aspired. The railings themselves caused an outcry across the country.[34]

Archbishop Laud saw Puritanism as a threat to the Church of England, and, fearing a schism in the Church, King Charles used the harsh measures of the Star Chamber to persecute religious dissenters. The punishments were horrific, and the illegality of the procedures, breaching ancient *habeas corpus* legislation, caused uproar amongst Puritans and Members of Parliament. Even those who did not support the Puritan cause were dismayed by Charles' punishments. Puritans would form the backbone of the Parliamentary forces opposing the repressive actions of King Charles I, often supported by families of 'old money' who had been snubbed by James I and Charles I, such as the Earls of Suffolk and the Earl of Bedford.[35]

The resulting conflict would bring England to Civil War.

----

34 Purkiss, 2006.

35 Sackville-West, 2010, gives a wonderful description of the build-up to the English Civil War, and the motivations of the different families choosing sides.

Chapter Seven

Declarations of War

Many story-tellers criticise Mary as a 'bad mother', neglecting her children at Fitzford[1], but during Sir Richard's five-year absence, Mary did try to spend time with her family, travelling frequently between Devon, Dorset and London[2] while running the Fitz estates, all the time writing to George Cutteford.

In her letters to George, Mary would affectionately address him as 'Honest Guts' or 'Good Guts'[3]. She would also teasingly call him 'Froward Guts', froward meaning obstinate, contrary or disobedient. 'Guts' may seem a strange nickname, but Mary was prone to using childish nicknames. She called her uncle Alexander Courtenay 'Sandr', for example. There is something

Okehampton Castle, from Britton's collection *Beauties of England and Wales*.

---

1 Miller, 1979, p. 38.
2 Radford, 1890, p. 84.
3 Radford, 1890.

about her name for George Cutteford that suggests she knew him from early childhood. 'Guts' is the kind of teasing epithet a child would use to a trusted friend, suggesting again, as other documents indicate, that George Cutteford had always been there for her, working with the family since she was born.

George Cutteford returned to Walreddon as Mary's steward, to oversee her lands in Devon and Cornwall, and entertain her friends. Theophilus Howard was a frequent visitor, enjoying the sports of the countryside in Cutteford's company. From his own hunting estate at Lulworth Castle in Dorset, Theophilus sent half a buck to Cutteford with many thanks for his 'noble entertainment', and wished he was back in Devon with his friend.[4] It's fascinating how often food was transported many miles as gifts between the landed gentry in the seventeenth century. Despite the logistics and cost, Lady Howard while in London frequently wrote to Cutteford requesting some game or poultry, with specific instructions for its preparations. One fine example is worth reproducing here:

> Honest Guts,
> You shall have a ton of wine to come, when mine does; and Mr... would have given me a hogshead of strong wine, but I told him he would do me a greater favour to make it for you, which he will do and send it you... I thank you for the letter, whose advice I wish I had ever followed, but awful experience has made me wiser. I thank you for my puddings, they are very good. I pray send me a whole flitch of bacon up, and some tongues and four turkeys, many boned and baked together, two one upon another with their breasts together, and piece of fat thin pork between them. So with my love to you, I rest,
> Your true friend till death,
> Mary Howard[5] [spelling improved for clarity]

---

4   Radford, 1890, p. 87.
5   Radford, 1890, p. 86.

Sadly, all the original letters are not to be found; they are currently not amongst the papers that survive from Cutteford's estate[6]. Cutteford's replies have also disappeared. However, the records that remain illuminate an affectionate friendship, and a woman of wealth busy about the daily affairs of her estates. What advice Cutteford offered, that Mary wished she had followed, is unfortunately lost to history, along with a clarification of what she means by 'fat thin pork'. Some things are best left to the imagination.

Mary's first letter to Cutteford was written while she was staying at the Earl of Suffolk's house in Dover; the second was sent from his Lulworth Castle in Dorset. Most show her anxious requests for news from Devon, which she viewed as her home. She rarely mentions the children by name, and sadly never mentions George Halse/Howard, though there is an implicit plea for information. Perhaps their son travelled with her. When she asks for news of the estate, there is a sense that she is as much – if not more – interested in the people she has left there than the properties themselves.

It is worth noting that Mary always signed herself Mary Howard, though she was still in fact Dame Mary Grenville, despite the 'divorce' proceedings.[7] Mary would spend the rest of her life disassociating herself, in vain, from her marriage with Sir Richard Grenville.

The letters that survive reveal a passionate lady who has not been well educated; her penmanship is very poor. This was not unusual, even for a woman of high rank. In The *Verneys*, by Adrian Tinniswood, the wealthy Verney girls, educated at home, are noted for their similarly poor penmanship.[8] A woman's education in the seventeenth century did not qualify her

6   Cutteford's surviving papers are currently held at West Sussex Record Office, in the manuscripts from Sackville College, Ref: Add Ms 18008. Mary Howard's letters are sadly no longer amongst them, so I rely on Mrs Radford's 1890 article for the Devonshire Association, where many of Mary Howard's letters are reproduced.

7   See Miller, 1979, p. 187n.

8   Tinniswood, 2007.

for serious writing – only for letters to family. Women were not educated with the aim of running a business or negotiating contracts; many women had to teach themselves even the basic paperwork required for running a household. As a result, Mary's spelling is inconsistent and often child-like in style. The son of a sailor was better educated than the wealthy woman who employed him.

Her other letters show that, although Sir Richard was absent, Mary still had trouble enough to vex her. The tenant at one of her properties in Milemead near Tavistock, called Tom Robinson, tormented her. Her uncle Alexander Courtenay ('Uncle Sandr') advised her to have the man arrested, but she could not bring herself to do so. Only one side of the conversation survives, as George's letters in reply sadly no longer exist, making it difficult to investigate the matter. But it is obvious from this brief letter that the Courtenays maintained an advisory role over Mary's business throughout her life.

In the letters that mention Tom Robinson, Mary writes with fear and trepidation. On route to Lulworth Castle, it seems, the widowed mother of Theophilus Howard was given a letter from someone called Tom Robinson, which the lady was instructed to pass to Lady Howard. Mary then wrote to Cutteford in great distraction, enclosing the letter from Tom Robinson (which strangely has been lost for centuries, it seems, perhaps deliberately[9]) and remarking that she is in such a state of terror that she dares not 'go abroad nor do anything'[10] until she has heard back from Cutteford, 'for he that values not his own life has yours or mine in his keeping. Wherefore, as you love me, take some such course with Tom Robinson, as I may never be troubled with him more.'[11]

---

9 The letter from Tom Robinson was not attached to Mary Howard's letters, when Mrs Radford was reading them in 1890. It was very likely deliberately destroyed by George Cutteford.

10 Radford, 1890, p. 87.

11 Radford, 1890, pp. 87 and 88.

Her next letter continues in the same ominous tone, asking Cutteford if he has:

> ...taken order with Tom Robinson, for I fear that mischievous man, whose.... lies cannot be imagined, will kill one of us: though there be never a true word in his letters, yet I fear he will do you or me some mortal harm, which I desire you to take the best course to avoid.[12]

The identity of Tom Robinson is lost to us, but it is intriguing that George Cutteford's daughter, Anne, married a Thomas Robinson, land agent to the Earl of Dorset. Robinson's business dealings for the Earl of Dorset meant he spent a great deal of time in the neighbourhood of Lulworth Castle. Cutteford would have found his daughter and her new husband a house near the Walreddon estate, as part of the marriage settlement, and Milemead is an ideal location. Is it possible that George Cutteford's son-in-law was threatening their lives?

During the English Civil War, one soldier was fiercely loyal to Sir Richard Grenville, a Lieutenant Colonel Thomas Robinson.[13] So loyal to Sir Richard, in fact, that this Thomas Robinson would do all he was bid – including kill for his master. Roger Granville, in his biography of Sir Richard Grenville, published in 1908[14], describes a Lieutenant-Colonel Robinson who, in the midst of the English Civil War, was ordered by his superiors not to burn Wellington House in Taunton. Lieutenant-Colonel Robinson then sought out his true master, Sir Richard, and subsequently burnt down Wellington House, despite orders to the contrary. Sir Richard commanded a loyalty in his men that overturned the

---

12 Radford, 1890, p. 88.

13 Miller, 1979, p. 149.

14 In 1908, Roger Granville published a biography of Sir Richard Grenville, entitled *The King's General in the West*, which, like Miller, 1979, describes the actions of Lieutenant-Colonel Thomas Robinson, and his loyalty to Sir Richard Grenville.

rulings of all other authorities. Perhaps Robinson's loyalties to
Sir Richard were established even before the English Civil War?

During the Civil War, Anne was separated from her husband, who then died sometime in the 1650s. Although it is
feasible neither of these men was the Tom Robinson in Mary's
letters, it is still interesting to conjecture that the source of
Mary's fear was George's son-in-law, who may have discovered
the true nature of George Halse's birth from his employer, the
Earl of Dorset.

Anne Cutteford's husband may have disapproved of his father-
in-law's immoral behaviour, and possibly threatened to denounce
the pair of them. Perhaps Tom Robinson wanted to blackmail
Cutteford and Mary Howard, or possibly he was just a disgruntled tenant, conceivably an ally of Sir Richard Grenville, who
went beyond the bounds of proper behaviour and unlawfully
threatened them with serious harm. Whoever Tom Robinson
was, George Cutteford must have dealt with him – probably
paying him off – as no more of the matter is mentioned.[15]

Instead, Mary's letters are subsequently filled with the worrying news of the return of Sir Richard Grenville. In 1638,
George Cutteford visited Mary in London, and her letters
indicate how thrilled she was to see him there again. Sadly,
however, they argued, and he left London without saying farewell. Mary's subsequent letter chides him, beginning 'Froward
Cutter'. She forgave him for not saying goodbye, describing
herself as 'now and ever his faithfullest friend'[16] and asking
'pray not be angry with me that loves you'. This may have
been the last time George and Mary saw each other, though
the subsequent records are incomplete. The return of Sir
Richard would tear them apart.

In January 1639, Sir Richard Grenville arrived back in
London. Decrees by the Star Chamber had been repealed[17]
so it seems that Sir Richard was safe from prosecution –

---

15 Radford, 1890, p. 89.

16 Radford, 1890, p. 89.

17 Miller, 1979, p. 40.

although he still owed Theophilus Howard £4,000, and another £4,000 to the King. Sir Richard declared he had returned to serve the King in the impending war between England and Scotland[18], and convinced King Charles that access to his old Fitz estates would enable him at last to pay off his fines. All these reasons are valid, and in accordance with Sir Richard's statements at the time – but in fact, Sir Richard returned primarily because news had reached him of the death of Sir Francis Courtenay.

In 1638, Sir Francis Courtenay died in mysterious circumstances, at just sixty-two years old. The matter of ownership of the Fitz estates, in particular the ownership of Okehampton Castle – and whether or not Sir Francis had inherited them from his father – had still not been settled, and the executors were faced with having to investigate the matter.[19] It seems the Courtenays lost their claim during the investigation.

Francis Courtenay's death left his eldest son, Sir William Courtenay, just nine years old[20], at the mercy of the Court of Wards. Fortunately for the young boy, his mother was Elizabeth Seymour, from a wealthy family herself, who soon re-married into the equally ancient Ameredith family, and so had the money available to purchase her son's guardianship.[21] This put oversight of Powderham Castle and all the Courtenay estates officially into the hands of Amos Ameredith for the duration of the wardship. The Ameredith family had recently sold their Slapton estates to the infamous Hawkins family, so access to the property and income from the Courtenay's estates must have been very welcome. The young Sir William, though, was

18 Miller, 1979, p. 40.

19 L1508M/Family/Testamentary Papers/3, 1639. Held at Devon Record Office.

20 Some records indicate Sir William Courtenary was only two years old at the time of his father's death in 1638; some say he was four. However, Sir William was about sixteen when Sir Richard had him arrested in 1644, so he must have been born in 1628/29.

21 D1508M/E/Accounts/V/29, held at Devon Record Office, is the account book of Lady Elizabeth Ameredith, guardian of Sir William Courtenay.

equally fortunate to be able to grow up with his mother and her new relations in comparative safety.

This sudden departure of his powerful adversaries, the Courtenays, was so much to Sir Richard's benefit that there could have been suspicions at the time of Grenville's involvement in the death of Sir Francis. Whatever the cause of death, Grenville took immediate advantage of the changing circumstances.

On his arrival in London, Sir Richard set about reclaiming the Fitz estates, with the support of his friend Philip Herbert, the 4th Earl of Pembroke, who was then one of the trustees of the Fitz estates. First, Sir Richard sued the Earl of Suffolk, Mary's brother-in-law, compelling him to pay the widow's jointure of £600 a year not to Mary Howard but to Sir Richard, still officially her husband.

Sir Richard wrote a long letter to the King's Council, outlining in detail how the Earl of Suffolk owed him £12,656, more than enough to pay Sir Richard's outstanding fines.[22] The fortunes of the Howards were still suffering from the downfall of previous Earl of Suffolk, Sir Thomas, with mounting debts at Audley End – a demand for nearly £13,000 was the last thing they needed. Relentlessly, Sir Richard petitioned the King and the Council, vowing 'never to leave petitioning until he had gained his will'.[23] Sir Richard had the Earl of Suffolk in his sights, with vengeance as his sole aim; nothing would distract him.

The battles in court had taken their toll on Theophilus Howard, 2nd Earl of Suffolk. By the end of June 1640, he was dead, at just fifty-eight years old, his eldest son, James, succeeding him as the 3rd Earl of Suffolk. The Howards would never again be a threat to the ambitions of Sir Richard Grenville.

Mary had lost her protector in London. She was already writing to George Cutteford of her financial difficulties. She wrote telling him she was struggling to pay for supplies of

---

22 Radford, 1890, p. 90.

23 Miller, 1979, p. 41.

wood to the house, and the rates which she was charged to aid the sick were overwhelming. It seems the plague had come to London and the surrounding districts, and 183 had died in Mary's parish just that week. Her neighbourhood seemed full of beggars.[24] The letter does not indicate her location – there is no way of knowing where she was living at the time, though she was probably staying at Rushey Green Place, her mansion in Lewisham. It seems strange that all sources of income had been lost to her, and she now relied solely on money being sent by George Cutteford from Devon. The amount she owed to creditors was rising drastically.

To make matters worse, in November 1640, Sir Richard Grenville had Mary declared an outlaw! She owed money to a man called Robert Fearebread[25] and the then Sheriff of Devon was required to produce Mary Howard (alias Grenville) in court. When she did not appear, she was declared an outlaw and the Sheriff of Devon was permitted to seize any of her goods or property in Devon to pay off the debt. No one seemed to know where she was. In 1640, Mary Howard went into hiding.

With his wife outlawed, Sir Richard Grenville re-claimed her property for himself. In December 1640, he went to Fitzford, expelled Mary's servants and reinstated his aunt, Catherine Abbot, as head of the household. Mary Howard was furious, writing to Cutteford of her desperation[26] but there was nothing George Cutteford could do. Cutteford himself was fortunate to avoid Grenville's wrath at that moment, for worse was soon to come.

At the same time, Scotland and England were at war, and Sir Richard found himself with a command in the King's army, marching north to Berwick in the spring of 1639, along-side his brother, Bevil Grenville. Scottish forces had invaded

24 Radford, 1890, p. 90.
25 D1508M/Moger/393. A writ of 1640, declaring Mary Howard an outlaw, held at Devon Record Office.
26 Radford, 1890, p. 90.

Northumberland as far as Newcastle, demanding freedom from the rulings of the English King and refusing to accept the new Book of Common Prayer. King Charles took his forces north to contest the invasion.

The Scottish armies were so strong and fiercely motivated, and the English so unprepared for war, that Charles was forced to make peace. The following year, Grenville was engaged again to counter the Scottish army, and achieved distinction. While most of the English troops at the Battle of Newburn fled in panic from the banks of the Tyne, Grenville and just a few other officers continued to oppose the Scottish charge across the river, at great personal risk, and refused to back away until the retreat had officially been called.

Whilst he found glory on the battlefield, Grenville's actions otherwise hinted at corruption. A young ensign called Cressy Dymocke complained to the Privy Council that, before the Battle of Newburn, Sir Richard Grenville had stopped his pay for a fortnight and charged him with receiving supplies that Dymocke had never seen. Perhaps Dymocke had some personal grievances, but the truth of his words is corroborated by another man's accusations that Sir Richard had received money from the King for new saddles, but had bought instead cheaper old saddles and pocketed the difference.[27] Wherever Grenville went, there was a hint of some financial misdealing. These charges, however, were ignored by King Charles I, who desperately needed Sir Richard Grenville for a greater, more vicious battle to come – in Ireland.

In February 1642, Sir Richard set sail for Dublin. During the previous year, thousands of English and Scottish Protestant settlers had been slaughtered there, amidst violent rebellion, and the early days of what would become known as the

---

27 Miller, 1979, p. 42.

Confederate Wars or the Eleven Years War.[28] Parliament had demanded that the King send forces to Ireland to protect the Protestant settlers there and defend the Protestant cause. By the time Sir Richard arrived, only Dublin and a few nearby towns still remained in English hands, under the forces of the Earl of Ormonde, surrounded and frequently besieged by overwhelming numbers of Irish rebels.

As always, Sir Richard showed his true colours in battle. In a cavalry skirmish near Waterford, in which thirty-five rebels died, Sir Richard personally captured a relative of a rebel leader. Grenville's cavalry scored another victory at the Battle of Kilrush, and in April 1642, he went northward from Dublin to County Meath, in an expedition under Sir Charles Coote. In Meath, their actions were brutal – they burned one town, and killed many rebel soldiers, including twenty-four whom they hanged. Charles Coote was notorious for his cruelty, frequently reported to have had children slaughtered 'so they would not grow up to be rebels like their parents'; even his own men protested.[29] The English forces went on to capture Trim on the 2 May 1642, slaying sixty of the enemy there. Grenville assumed command at Trim following the death of Charles Coote, and fought off a major assault, securing the town.

Trim was a vital location for the defence of Dublin, having an important strategic position in the Pale, the historic area around Dublin that had been the centre of English power in Ireland for centuries. But the defences of Trim were in a poor state, which Sir Richard urgently addressed within limited resources – lacking suitable labourers (then called 'pioneers'), his soldiers had to perform the menial task of repairing the fortifications themselves, against the threat of siege by the increasing rebel forces.

---

28 Miller, 1979. Also see http://www.british-civil-wars.co.uk/military/confederate-war.htm. The people of Ireland appear to have been constantly in the midst at war during the sixteenth and seventeenth centuries, mostly fighting the invading English. Tinniswood, 2007, also gives an excellent account of the battles in Ireland.

29 Miller, 1979, p. 61.

Within the town were many who did not support the English cause, but the rebel sympathisers were soon to discover the brutal nature of Sir Richard's control. At the first hint of unrest, the entire population of Trim were forced to appear before Sir Richard, under threat of execution, and with help from informers, Sir Richard identified about 100 rebel sympathisers, forty of whom he immediately expelled from the town. One woman who was exiled was heard to wish all the English hanged – so Sir Richard had her and her maid hanged in the centre of Trim, as a warning to the remaining inhabitants. Sir Richard was not a man to be crossed.

The next few months Sir Richard spent harrying the enemy. In May he made a surprise attack on a nearby town, probably Maynooth[30]; the inhabitants so surprised and terrified that many fled from their beds carrying their clothes. He then besieged Maynooth Castle, which succumbed after just one hour, and he put all 100 defenders to the sword. Ironically, this became known as the Maynooth Pardon.[31]

At another castle, the Irish rebels scorned all quarter and hurled stones down upon Sir Richard's forces. After many days, Grenville's cannon finally breached the walls, and the Irish forces retreated to the upper levels, setting fire to the ground floors to resist the breach. Finally defeated, the survivors emerged from the castle, about 140 of them, many of them women and children. Of these, sixty of the men were stripped, killed and left unburied, as a warning to any further insurrections.

The contemporary stories of the Irish rebellions were filled with atrocities, albeit often exaggerated to appeal to the English masses in their cry for forces to defend the Protestant cause in Ireland. This campaign of embellished claims and counter-claims was typical of the seventeenth century, enduring throughout the English Civil War, so it is often difficult to rely on contemporary news stories as facts. However,

---

30 Miller, 1979, p. 44.

31 The history of Maynooth Castle, at http://www.kildare.ie/heritage/historic-sites/maynooth-castle.asp describes the Maynooth Pardon.

Sir Richard's horrific reputation in Ireland is confirmed by personal accounts at the time. Some stories of his cruelty would have been circulated by Sir Richard himself in an attempt to subdue the local population, but many stories from his allies have survived, and are good evidence of Sir Richard's cruel nature, especially in his treatment of prisoners of war. Grenville's form of justice became known as 'Trim Law', and he himself would boast about his callous actions, and how he was accountable to no one but himself.

Despite his barbaric methods, Sir Richard's troops remained fiercely loyal to him. Most admired him as a hard fighting man battling in harsh times, willing to do whatever was necessary to win against often impossible odds. In turn, Sir Richard remained loyal to his men, always taking great pains to see them fed and supplied as well as possible. He had learned a great deal from the mistakes made at the Cadiz expedition of 1625, he demanded discipline from his men, and in return ensured they were adequately supplied – adequately, of course, but perhaps not as well as they could have been, as the story of the saddles shows. To buy the loyalty of his men, Sir Richard was renowned for raising the funds by robbing old women and hanging bedridden old men when they would not tell him where their money was hidden.[32] Sir Richard would continue to employ such dishonourable methods for the remainder of his fighting career. But buying loyalty did not bring him the support of all of his men.

While the area around Dublin was devastated by the English armies, in an attempt to starve out the Irish rebels, and thereby also bringing starvation to the inhabitants of Dublin, Sir Richard, in contrast, made allies of the farmers around Trim, allowing them to hold markets in the town and maintain a flourishing trade. He defended this policy to his superiors, reasonably arguing that his farming allies were now more apt to betray the rebels to him.

---

32 Miller, 1979, p. 61.

However, the rebels themselves managed to burn all the corn and forage around Trim, forcing Grenville's men to travel more than 7 miles for food and fuel. The constant drain on manpower, with illness and desertion reducing his forces at one time to less than 500 men, left the town very prone to siege. While rebuilding the fortifications, mutiny became an issue, with frequent battles over food – Grenville had to imprison one of his own captains for stealing some cows.

While Grenville was visiting his superiors in Dublin, one of his majors and some of the men stole food from Grenville's quarters, leaving the remaining troops without any supplies, and Grenville on his return had to have the culprits banished. The departing hungry soldiers attacked their armed escort and stole away with cattle, corn and bedding. Meanwhile, other vital supplies were being sold illegally outside the town. Sir Richard's methods did not ensure absolute loyalty.

Amidst the calamities, and with the diminishing resources and fighting men, Grenville did manage to maintain his attacks on the rebels, constantly informing his superiors of his victories; however, eventually Grenville's convoy to supply Dublin was attacked, with twelve of his men killed and 160 cows taken by the rebels. Grenville's position in Ireland remained precarious.

Meanwhile, in London, in October 1642, Mary Howard sent her last surviving letter to George Cutteford:

Honest Guts,
I pray as ever you love me, send me a bill for 20 pounds, for God knows whether I shall live to have any more. Here is such hurliburly and all commodities are taken up, and this day the city has taken up all the provisions from the country people, that the suburbs can hardly provide themselves. Each man provides, that is able, for a quarter of a year. Mrs G... is going out of town, for her husband sent her a letter so to do. For my part I fear nothing but want of money. The King's army is a day's march before his citizens. The King was yesterday five miles this side of Oxford. Mr C.... wearies

me to death for money. I pray, as you respect me, send me
a bill of exchange for 20 pounds....All the shops are commanded to be shut up, so in haste I rest.

Your true friend,
Mary Howard

[Post script] The report here is that the armies have met, but
no certainty who is killed, but I believe my Lord of Essex
has the worse because I hear no crying of good news.[33]

And so began the English Civil War. The first battle, at
Edgehill, described in uncertain terms by Mary Howard, had
resulted in a stalemate between the Royalist forces of King
Charles I and Parliament's Army, led by the Earl of Essex, Sir
Robert Devereux. Royalist forces on their way to London to
support the King found their path intercepted by Essex's army
at Edgehill, an escarpment in Warwickshire. The battle raged
for three hours, with heavy losses on both sides – 1,000 dead
and nearly 3,000 wounded. The Parliamentary forces finally
withdrew to a garrison in Warwick. King Charles decided
to take his remaining army slowly to London, via Oxford,
Aylesbury and Reading, probably to recruit men and secure
supplies, on his way to what he saw as his glorious advance
to re-take London, but Essex's forces beat them to the capital.
Both sides effectively lost the battle, achieving nothing, and
London remained in the hands of Parliament.

THE GHOSTS OF EDGEHILL

The following year, reports reached King Charles of ghosts
haunting the Edgehill battlefield.[34] He was so intrigued by

33 Radford, 1890, p. 92.
34 For one description of the ghosts of Edgehill, see http://en.wikipedia.org/
    wiki/Edge_Hill,_Warwickshire

the numerous eyewitness accounts that he sent two reliable representatives, who had fought with him at Edgehill, to investigate – and they too witnessed the battle re-enacted in ghostly form before their eyes. In subsequent years, even during the Civil War, many visited Edgehill to watch the ghosts do battle, though the ghostly soldiers seem to have faded over the centuries. Even now, however, visitors do sometimes hear the sounds of the fighting and the cries of the wounded and dying at the site, the spectral echo of the last moments of the men so pointlessly slain at Edgehill.

King Charles, unable to enter London, established his new headquarters at Oxford, with his own separate Parliament, for the duration of the Civil War. George Cutteford's old friend, the Earl of Dorset, joined the King there, first continuing his role as Lord Chamberlain to the Queen, then in 1644 taking on the role of Lord Chamberlain to the King himself. As Lord Chamberlain, Dorset was responsible for the business of the royal household, and acted as King Charles I's spokesman in Oxford in the King's absence. This was a role that would play an important part in George Cutteford's future.

Mary Howard would not be heard from again until 1644.[35] Her whereabouts remained unknown, and personal communications between London and other parts of the country became fraught with problems. If she wrote to Cutteford again, still in Devon, the letters might never have reached him. The country was divided on all levels, by geography, by battle-lines, by religion and politics; families were separated, loyalties torn apart and the land stripped of resources to feed and supply the tens of thousands of men marshalled into the opposing armies.

However, there must have been some communications between Lady Howard and the Cuttefords. In 1642, she agreed to supply funds for George's eldest son to receive a

---

35 Radford, 1890.

commission in Drake's regiment.[36] At the commencement of the war, Sir William Russell, Earl of Bedford – and Mary's cousin – was appointed by Parliament to be Lord Lieutenant of Devon, responsible for the recruitment of Devon men into Parliament's armies. One of the first regiments was formed by Sir Francis Drake, a nephew of the famous sea captain, who still lived in Tavistock. This young Sir Francis gathered together a team of cavalrymen, which would be known as the Plymouth Horse, fighting in most of the major battles of the south-west region. It is very likely that George Cutteford the younger, and possibly his brother John, were amongst them.

Drake's Plymouth Horse are mentioned in descriptions of the Battle of Sourton Down, which took place in April 1643, just south west of Okehampton. Having unsuccessfully battled against the Royalist forces in Cornwall, at Launceston, the Parliamentary forces, under Major General Chudleigh, fell back into Devon, drawing the Royalist forces after them. As the King's men approached Okehampton, Chudleigh led a small cavalry force into a surprise attack on the Royalists at Sourton Down. At the same time, Captain Drake[37] charged his cavalry against the advance guard of Royalist dragoons, who panicked and fell back against their own troops behind them. After some fierce fighting, the Parliamentary army was eventually repelled, but were then reinforced by 1,000 men from Okehampton, attacking the Royalists who had taken up defensive positions along ancient earthworks on the moor.

As the skirmishing continued into the night, a violent storm drenched the combatants, causing further terror and confusion, and the Royalists pulled out, leaving behind weapons, gunpowder and important letters between the King and the

---

36 Radford, 1890, p. 101.

37 This Captain Drake may have been Thomas Drake, brother to Sir Francis Drake, both nephews to the legendary privateer, Sir Francis Drake. The brothers Thomas and Francis both fought for Parliament, for the Plymouth garrison and were involved in battles in the South West. From Radford, 1890, p. 101, it is difficult to identify for which Drake George Cutteford the younger was fighting.

leaders of the Royalist forces. After their King's success in Cornwall, this disordered retreat was an embarrassment for the Royalists. Drake's Plymouth Horse proved to be a significant asset for Parliament throughout the war.

Still fighting in Ireland, Sir Richard was proving more successful than his King, though bad weather was a constant adversary. In late January 1643, Grenville's forces – 1,000 infantry and 200 cavalry – were sent to supply Athlone in the heart of Ireland. While there, Sir Richard's men killed many civilians, and, in violation of a treaty, raided the lands of the rebel leader Sir James Dillon.

Returning with 600 soldiers from the English garrison at Athlone, many of whom were sick, starving or wounded and who died on the journey, Sir Richard was determined to make his way directly to Trim. Unfortunately this meant travelling via a pass near Rathconnell, over a deep trench with marshes on either side. The pass, Grenville discovered, was held by an Irish force of about 4,000 men.

Grenville sent an advance guard, a 'forlorn hope' of musketeers, to attempt the pass, but they failed, despite reinforcements. According to Grenville himself[38], he then made a brave and stirring speech to the remaining men, telling them to take the pass or die. The men battled on for two hours, both sides suffering casualties, only to be interrupted by a severe hailstorm. Suddenly, a rain-soaked swamp separated Grenville's forces from the enemy and the disputed pass. Two officers eventually managed to find a passage through the marsh with a troop of horse, and slowly Grenville's army reached the crossing, still under fire from rebel musketeers. When their ammunition ran out, the rebels hurled stones at the English troops, but their forces were finally dispersed by the sheer ferocity of Grenville's men, who massacred the retreating rebel forces for miles around; 250 Irish rebels were killed, not a large percent-

---

38 Miller, 1979, p. 56.

age of the initial force, but still large in contrast to Grenville's reported losses of just three men.

Grenville took prisoner eleven rebels, and four days later he and his troops paraded them through Dublin. One contemporary observer commented on the ragged and sick condition of Grenville's victorious men. Parliament in London declared Grenville's actions at Rathconnell to be one of the greatest victories in Ireland since the wars began.[39] At last Grenville was a hero – at least to the English.

Battling in England and desperate for heroic, effective leaders for his armies, King Charles invited his nephews from Europe, Princes Rupert and Maurice, to take charge of much of his campaign. News of Sir Richard Grenville's heroic deeds in Ireland would have delighted King Charles – Sir Richard was just the kind of leader the King urgently needed.

Funds for the wars in Ireland were dwindling. In April 1643, there were riots in Dublin as unpaid English soldiers plundered the local populace. King Charles I could no longer raise funds through Parliament, and instead decided to negotiate a truce in Ireland, so he could concentrate on his battles in England. The negotiations would be held at Trim, leaving Sir Richard bitter and angry – he was very unhappy with the new policy, and was subsequently ordered by the King to return to England.

King Charles was elated to have Sir Richard, the national hero, return to join his battles against Parliament. In late August 1643, Sir Richard made his way home across the Irish Sea, but Parliament were ready for the return of this famous Royalist. They met him on the docks in Liverpool and immediately put Grenville and his friends under arrest for his allegiance to the King.

But Sir Richard would surprise them all. This national hero, brought back to England by the King himself, publicly declared he had returned to fight against the King. Instead, Sir Richard chose to fight for Parliament.

---

39 Miller, 1979, p. 57.

Chapter Eight

Triumph of a Traitor

ir Richard and his col-
leagues on returning from
Ireland had intended to
land in Royalist-held Chester,
but the ship containing all their
goods was captured and taken
to Parliament's Liverpool garrison. Not wanting to lose his
belongings, and in particular
his money, Grenville arrived
in Liverpool to ensure his
goods were not plundered
by Parliament's Roundhead
soldiers. Once there, despite
Grenville's protests, he and his
friends were arrested and transported to London under guard.

Parliament had every reason
to be suspicious of Sir Richard.
His elder brother, Sir Bevil
Grenville, had been the brave
and dedicated heart of the

Oliver Cromwell.

King's army in Devon and Cornwall, afforded steadfast loyalty
by his men, and accolades for his bravery. Leading his Cornish
pikemen to great victory at the Battle of Lansdown in July
1643, Sir Bevil had been fatally wounded. Parliament and King
Charles I would no doubt have thought that Sir Richard had

returned in August 1643 out of familial love to replace his late brother in the King's forces, fighting for the glory of the King. But Sir Richard Grenville was of another breed entirely.

With funds in short supply, the King had not been able to afford to pay Sir Richard and many other officers for their services in Ireland, for some time. Parliament, however, had made a grandiose offer to reimburse all those returning from Ireland, if they joined the Parliamentary cause. To Sir Richard, the money was an excellent incentive. So when Grenville was summoned to the House of Commons, under arrest, he declared, much to everyone's astonishment and the delight of the Parliamentary leaders, he would never serve against Parliament, and chose to serve against the Queen in defence of the Protestant religion.

According to a contemporary diarist, Walter Yonge[1], Richard Grenville also said he would never serve against the King, but this ambiguity appears to have been lost on his audience, who immediately reimbursed him the monies owing from his services in Ireland, and offered him an appointment as Lieutenant-General of Horse, under Sir William Waller, fighting for Parliament.

Enchanted with their gallant soldier, there was also talk of appointing Sir Richard Grenville as the Governor of Plymouth, which was then one of the few remaining and most important Parliamentary garrisons in the south west, though besieged by the King's forces. As a Grenville, an ancient and local family, Parliament's officials felt he was sure to recruit more of the population of Cornwall and Devon to the Parliamentary cause. In anticipation, Sir Richard spent a great deal of their money on his attire and other equipage – his taste for fine shirts had certainly not abated.[2] Some people at the time questioned whether this was an appropriate use of Parliament's dwindling resources.

---

1   Miller, 1979, p. 65.
2   Miller, 1979, p. 66.

Arriving to take up his post in the army of Sir William Waller, however, his enthusiasm seems to have waned. His new associates were Puritans and independent preachers who denounced swearing, drinking, womanising and raucous behaviour of any sort, and demanded that all adhered to the Sabbath and attended church services regularly, often more than once a day. In short, his new-found allies had taken all the fun out of warfare. Richard was not to suffer it for long.

Not realising Grenville's change of heart, Sir William Waller, having the highest regard for Grenville's abilities as an officer, took him into his complete confidence. Waller had been a great admirer of Sir Bevil Grenville, despite their opposing political views, and Waller expected Sir Richard similarly to be a man of honour. Waller could not have been more wrong.

Sir William confided in Richard all his military plans – their first objective was to take Basing House in Hampshire. The Royalist commander at Basing House had offered to give up the garrison, and Sir Richard was to take his cavalry there for a 'surprise attack' in preparation for Waller's arrival. Sir Richard duly set out from London on 2 March 1644, with a rather opulent train of coaches and horses, soldiers and servants, and £600 from Parliament for further recruitment on the way. His procession travelled under a magnificent banner; a map of England and Wales on a crimson background, with the words 'England Bleeding' in golden letters across the top. The Puritans of London cheered him on, enjoying the spectacle, with Sir Richard acknowledging their support with a wave and a fixed smile. Mary Howard may even have been among the crowd.

Rallying at Bagshot, Sir Richard then made an astonishing declaration – he told all his men that he was in fact a Royalist, and was changing sides; taking most of his entourage – and all of the money – he headed for Oxford to meet the King.

The King was overjoyed to receive his prodigal soldier, and even more pleased to hear of Parliament's plans to attack Basing House. The traitorous officer in charge at Basing House was arrested, and the Royalist garrison was saved.

Parliament was left enraged and embarrassed. Sir Richard wrote a letter to the Speaker of the House of Commons, trying to explain his change of heart, but his insulting descriptions of the nature and composition of their Puritan forces merely infuriated Parliament. In response, the leaders of Parliament had two gibbets erected, at the Palace Yard in Westminster and at the Royal Exchange, with the proclamation:

> Whereas Sir Richard Grenville hath of late presented his service unto the Parliament and hath been entertained by the Parliament as Colonel of a regiment of horse; and whereas the said Grenville, contrary to his promise, engagement and honour as a soldier hath basely, unworthily and faithlessly deserted the said service and feloniously carried away the money paid unto him for the said service – these are to proclaim the said Grenville traitor, rogue, villain and skellum not only incapable of military employment but of all acquaintance and conversation with men of honesty and honour.[3]

Sir Richard would be known as 'Skellum Grenville' for the rest of his life, skellum meaning a rogue or rascal. Plymouth, commanded by Parliament's forces and under siege by the Royalists, would soon resound with furious oaths directed at that 'Skellum Grenville'.

Sadly, Grenville's desertion occurred just as the King was proposing a peace treaty between his Oxford Parliament and the 'rebels' at Westminster. On the 9 March, however, the Westminster Parliament rejected a call for peace talks, and refused to recognise the legitimacy of the Oxford Parliament. No doubt they were still embittered and upset by Grenville's traitorous behaviour and felt they couldn't trust the King either.

As a reward to Grenville for his loyalty, the King sequestered all of the properties of the so-called outlaw Lady Howard and awarded them at last to Sir Richard, who was happily sent

---

3   Miller, 1979, pp. 69 and 70.

into Devon and Cornwall to recruit men there to the Royalist
cause. Sir Richard's recruitment drive would have to wait,
however. First, he had a far more important task to perform.

In mid-March 1644, Sir Richard duly reported to Prince
Maurice, the King's nephew, who was in charge of the Royalist
forces in the south west. Prince Maurice's army was then sta-
tioned in Tavistock, having successfully subdued the town's
Puritan population, many of whom, including the Puritan
minister George Hughes, had been forced to abandon their
homes and taken refuge in Parliament's Plymouth garrison.

Sir Richard's first act under the King was to have Prince
Maurice draw up a warrant for the arrest of his old enemy
George Cutteford. The grounds for the arrest were that
Cutteford had received large sums of money from lands now
belonging to Sir Richard – though the charges were highly
questionable, considering Sir Richard had had no oversight of
the properties for some years. The warrant was presented by
Sir Richard to the local Provost Marshall, overseeing all disci-
plinary matters in the armed forces, and a troop of soldiers was
sent to Walreddon to arrest George Cutteford and throw his
family off the property. Sir Richard probably personally supervised the arrest. His revenge had been a long time coming.

It was a bleak day in March 1644 for George Cutteford
and his wife. Sir Richard and his men moved swiftly, quickly
travelling the mile from Tavistock along the winding roads to
Walreddon to surprise its residents.

Until that moment, George Cutteford had managed
to remain out of the war, living quietly with his wife at a
distance from the calamities affecting Tavistock. His sons
George and John were away from home, battling against the
Royalists; his daughters had all married and moved away; so
it was just George Cutteford the elder, now in his fifties, and
his wife Grace at home with the servants when Sir Richard's
small troop of horse arrived. They hammered on the back
door of Walreddon, the one facing the road, and dragged
Cutteford away.

Some say they immediately took Cutteford to Exeter to be imprisoned there at Rougemont Castle[4], but the local Provost Marshall had no jurisdiction there, and the nearest gaol was Lydford. Lydford Gaol had been notorious for generations, and now it was George Cutteford who was brought in chains before the warden, and sent down the 30ft ladder into the black windowless pit below. His friends and family would not know where to look for him. It was in the pit of Lydford Gaol that Sir Richard Grenville wanted George Cutteford to die.

LYDFORD GAOL

Lydford Castle was established as the gaol for the Stannaries in 1305. It had been built as a prison in 1195, as the centre of administration for Dartmoor, with its own courthouse, and subsequently the Stannary Court regularly sent criminals to be held at Lydford. Most crimes involved debt or the theft of tin or other metals, though in 1306 a tin miner called Walter Wallyngs was imprisoned at Lydford for murder. Over the centuries, many tinners found their way to Lydford Gaol[5], with local people frequently protesting the incarceration of friends and relatives. At first, the building was said to be in satisfactory condition, and a payment to the gaoler could often afford some comfort, but by the sixteenth century the prison had fallen into disrepair and was described as the most detestable place in England.

Many complained of the misconduct of the gaolers, starving the prisoners and treating them brutally. In the early seventeenth century, Richard Foster from Ugborough reported his gaolers to the Star Chamber, following his imprisonment at Lydford. Foster described being lowered into a dungeon, a filthy pit, with no light or chance of a fire

---

4   Radford, 1890, p. 94 implies that Cutteford was sent straight to Exeter, though she and Miller, 1979, do not name the gaol where Cutteford was held.

5   Greeves, 2005.

for heat. The floor beneath the wall where he was chained was just a few boards suspended over a 30ft deep pit well in the western corner. It was a terrifying prospect for any man who lost his footing in the pitch dark.

In 1638, King Charles I sent funds and supplies of wood for repairs to be made to Lydford Gaol. Perhaps he intended to have conditions there improved, but his motives were also to ensure that the gaol remained a secure and terrifying prospect to anyone who might consider stealing from his mines. Money was his prime motivation; certainly not the comfort of his prisoners. Lydford Castle remained the stuff of nightmares.

The horror of Lydford Gaol culminated in the arrival of Sir Richard Grenville in 1644, infamous for his cruelty to the prisoners. Scores of innocent men from Tavistock died at Lydford, at the hands of Grenville's gaolers. Contemporary accounts describe travelling the road past Lydford to hear the cries of men, desperate for food and water, dying slowly in the decrepit and noxious castle. Located in what was at one time a substantial town on the edge of Dartmoor, just off the road between Tavistock and Okehampton, it was never more than a square stone fortress, a few storeys over basement dungeons, but for hundreds of men it became their final resting place. John Bond in January 1645 described Lydford prison:

In this prison, diverse debtors have been starved, and some were said to eate their own flesh, even in those times of peace and plenty. Guesse yee then, what cries and yells for bread and water there are now to be heard amongst the many scores which at present are shut up in that straight prison? Yea, the passengers doe heare the cries, ere they see the prison...[6]

---

6   Greeves, 2005, p. 10.

The neighbouring Castle Inn is said to be haunted by gaolers from Lydford, unable to leave as penance for the horrors of their actions. The last man to die at Lydford was left in chains on the outer walls, his body coated in pitch to preserve it, as a warning to everyone of the consequences of crossing Sir Richard Grenville.[7]

Sir Richard's revenge against Cutteford was just the first of his barbaric actions in Devon. He set about avenging himself against all his former enemies and their friends, and at the same time making as much money as possible. The more men died, the more Grenville's fortunes prospered.

Having imprisoned Cutteford, Sir Richard then sought out a man called Brabant who had acted as an attorney on behalf of Mary Howard and the Earl of Suffolk in their court battles against him. Mr Brabant was soon discovered, desperately trying to escape Devon in disguise: he was wearing a monteroe, a hunting cap made of Spanish cloth often worn by the Royalist soldiers. But Sir Richard recognised him in the street and immediately had him hanged as a spy. Sir Richard's Royalist allies questioned his motives for the summary execution, but Mr Brabant was probably still working for the Earl of Suffolk, then James Howard, who was fighting for Parliament; Sir Richard was probably right in his assumptions that Brabant was a spy. However, it was a brutal killing and both sides were horrified by Sir Richard's actions.

At the same time, Sir Richard decided to raise some much-needed money by kidnapping wealthy men, locking them up in Lydford Gaol and ransoming them back to their families. He also locked up hundreds of enemy soldiers there, including Lieutenant-Colonel James Halse, a distant relation of George Cutteford, who had been fighting on the side of Parliament. It was said that Richard Grenville personally visited

7   Mildren, 1987.

Lydford to try to convince James Halse to change sides, but when James refused, Sir Richard left him there to starve to death.

The Tavistock poet William Browne visited his friend James Halse there in 1644, and, horrified by the conditions and the imminent death of his friend, he wrote the famous words:'I oft have heard of Lydford law/ How in the morn they hang and draw/ And sit in judgement after.'[8]

Sir Richard's reputation for murder and plundering grew rapidly. Having failed to make his money through marriage and the courts, he now immersed himself in a life of the worst kind of piracy. And with the country locked in Civil War, there was no one to stop him. The King needed hard men to fight his war, and gave Sir Richard full rein to do as he pleased. Richard knew he was accountable to no one but himself now and took full advantage of his new situation.

Sir Richard sequestered the property of the Earl of Bedford, Sir William Russell, who was at that time working for Parliament, and reclaimed all of his wife's property around Tavistock, despite the protests of the Courtenays.

The young Sir William Courtenay, just sixteen, and his kins-man Peter Courtenay happened to be amongst the Royalist forces then besieging nearby Plymouth, and when Sir William objected to Sir Richard Grenville at the loss of what he saw as his property, including Fitzford manor, Sir Richard had the poor boy arrested and taken to Exeter in chains.

While Sir Richard ransacked Tavistock, nearby Plymouth was under siege by Royalist forces under the command of Sir Kenneth Digby. Digby invited his ally to dine with him. On his return from Digby's house, escorted by a few Royalist cavalry-men, Grenville encountered a small number of Parliamentary soldiers foraging for fuel. In an infamous episode, Sir Richard ordered one of the Parliamentary soldiers to hang his fellows from the nearest tree. Sir Richard contentedly watched, enjoy-

---

8 Greeves, 2005, p. 10.

ing the spectacle. Once the horrible task was completed, Sir
Richard got down from his horse and hanged the last man
himself. Again, Grenville's Royalist allies were horrified, realising that Sir Richard had brought 'Trim Law' back with him
from Ireland.

Sir Richard was a man of consequence without a con-
science – the war was turning him into a monster. Hanging
Englishmen without trial, even the enemy, was seen as a barbaric and unnecessary cruelty, but still the King continued his
support for his heroic General. Sir Richard's taste for vengeance did not end there.

Sir Kenneth Digby was wounded in a fierce skirmish against
the Plymouth garrison, and command of the Royalist forces
subsequently fell to Sir Richard. The Plymouth garrison had
successfully held out against the Royalists since war had been
declared in 1642, having been making preparations for such a
siege from as early as 1640. Its predominantly Puritan population
saw their fight against King Charles as a godly war, and they held
out even as the rest of Devon was overrun with Royalist soldiers.

As refugees fled to Plymouth from all over Devon, joined by
soldiers arriving from London to defend the town, the population of Plymouth swelled to over 8,000. The town was then
located in the square mile that is the 'old town' of the Barbican
today, around Sutton Pool docks.

Grace Cutteford and her family were probably among
the swelling population, having, like many, fled the terror of
Richard Grenville. Repeatedly the leat that brought fresh
water[9] was blocked by Royalist forces, and disease became a
constant threat, but Plymouth's population worked tirelessly,
men, women and children alike, repairing earthworks, feeding
and supplying the soldiers defending the forts, and tending
the wounded.

9   The legendary privateer Sir Francis Drake had a leat built to draw fresh water
    from Dartmoor into Plymouth, for his own benefit as much as anyone else's,
    the leat taking water to the mills. Sections of the old leat still survive between
    Yelverton and north Plymouth.

The overcrowded people of Plymouth were desperate, but not defeated, as the Plymouth harbour was so wide that Royalist cannon could not prevent Parliament's ships entering the port, bringing with them much needed supplies and reinforcements from London. As ships from Plymouth regularly attacked Royalist vessels along the south-west coast, the Royalists desperately needed to take Plymouth and so destroy this Parliamentary stronghold.

On 18 March 1644, Sir Richard sent a letter to the Governor at Plymouth, impressing upon the people of Plymouth the insecurity of their situation, and urging them to surrender. They refused, rejecting any quarter from 'Skellum Grenville' and announcing that they would rather have him as their enemy than their ally – a direct attack on his treacherous behaviour just a few weeks earlier.

During the next four months, Sir Richard ordered numerous attacks against the Plymouth garrison, with little success. The Plymouth forces had had plenty of time to establish a line of forts north of the town, along a natural ridge that runs 4 miles east to west. The names of the forts still resound in areas of Plymouth, such as Pennycomequick, Lipson and Maudley (now called Mutley Plain).

Between the forts, the Plymouth garrison built substantial earthworks, so even when desperately short of men they were able successfully to repel Grenville's attacks. Sir Richard battled on, but Plymouth stood its ground, frequently having great success in their own sorties against smaller Royalist forces in precarious outposts surrounding the harbour.

The Royalists set about plundering Plympton, to the south east of Plymouth, and the Plymouth garrison sent two units of horse and foot soldiers to attack them. George Cutteford the younger was probably amongst them. The Parliamentary forces managed to kill sixty of Sir Richard's men and captured 100 others. On their return to Plymouth they were pursued by Sir Richard and his men, but he was also beaten back, nearly getting himself killed in the attempt.

Sir Richard's lack of success probably stemmed from a shortage of men and supplies. Other battles in the south west were frequently drawing Royalist forces away from the siege, while the Plymouth garrison could often boast 3,000 soldiers. Sir Richard's forces were never large enough to counter that number. Sir Richard sent begging letters to his friends, including Edward Seymour, Governor of Dartmouth, in his desperate need for reinforcements and weaponry.

While Sir Richard was locked in a stalemate at Plymouth, he was shocked by news that Parliament's army was heading into the west with a force of 8,000 men commanded by the Earl of Essex. To counter the attack, Prince Maurice gathered a Royalist army at Okehampton, depleting Grenville's forces at Plymouth. But rather than face the Royalists at Okehampton, Essex cleverly turned south and rapidly headed for Plymouth instead. One of the most surprising aspects of the Civil War is just how fast an army of 8,000 with heavy artillery could move across the country.

Sir Richard, outnumbered, had less than four days to remove his men from his outposts in Tavistock and around Plymouth and retreat to Cornwall, but for some reason he delayed his retreat for as long as possible – he was very nearly taken by Essex. Once in Cornwall, Grenville set about recruiting troops and stealing whatever horses and arms he could find. Throughout the Civil War, horses were a valuable and frequently rare commodity.

Essex's forces reached Tavistock in July 1644, where Grenville had hurriedly left a garrison of 150 of his men at Fitzford. Essex immediately attacked the house and, although the garrison tried to surrender, waving a white flag, Essex blasted the house with cannon and his men stormed the building. They plundered anything and everything of any value.

Essex is said to have then made his way to Lydford to release the Parliamentary prisoners there – but George Cutteford, it seems, was not amongst them.

Sadly, Cutteford was already on his way to Exeter. It must have been an odd day for Sir William Courtenay, still languishing in Rougemont Castle in Exeter, when his family's agent was dragged into the cells, in chains. Why Cutteford was transferred to Rougemont at that time may never be known. Perhaps Richard Grenville, on hearing the news of Exeter's approach, had hastily had George moved to Exeter, a more secure location taken by the Royalists the year before, after a long siege.

Grenville certainly didn't want Cutteford released by the Parliamentary forces. He might even have delayed his retreat specifically to clear Lydford Gaol of any embarrassing prisoners, especially any Royalist allies still held for ransom. The Governor of Exeter, Sir John Berkeley, a loyal Royalist, may have simply requested that Cutteford be transferred from Lydford to Exeter, but his reasons remain lost to history.

For Cutteford, though, Rougemont Castle was no better than Lydford Gaol. Rougemont too was a detestable prison, cold, damp and dark. Food in Exeter remained scarce, now the city was frequently under siege by Parliament, and in the overcrowded houses, disease was rife. At least George Cutteford was away from the tormenting guards at Lydford, no longer daily threatened with summary execution – many were often hanged without trial at Lydford, just because they were running out of food. At least Cutteford was less likely to be executed in Exeter – if he didn't die of starvation or disease first.

For four long months, George Cutteford had heard nothing of his family, or of whether they were alive or dead. Cutteford had watched others die around him at Lydford: many were tortured and hanged, and he knew that he was lucky still to be alive, but the fate of his family must have been ever-present in his thoughts. He knew his sons were fighting for Parliament, and that Sir Richard Grenville was eager to find them and have them killed, but he had no idea of the horrors they were to suffer.

Plymouth sent 2,000 men to join Essex's army, now a force of over 8,000 that probably included George Cutteford's sons.

Their mood was optimistic, confident that this was the army that would re-take Devon and Cornwall from the Royalists. Essex's forces, joined by Lord Robartes from Plymouth, chased the retreating Grenville into Cornwall. Parliament was delighted with Essex's success, one commentator declaring:

> His excellency under the conduct of the noble, honest and active Lord Robartes sent a party of horse into Cornwall to pursue the running, run-away Grenville, who flies like guilty Cain from every shadow, frightened by his fancies and tormented by a prickling, galled conscience for symptoms of misery, a hell within and a halter at Westminster that makes the man as mad as a March hunted hare.[10]

In fact, nothing could have been further from the truth, for Grenville was drawing Essex into an ambush. Pursuing Grenville, Essex suddenly found the King and his army of 10,000 behind him, approaching from the east. Essex's forces were suddenly trapped by Royalist armies on all sides.

In July 1644, the King made a brief stop in Exeter. The previous month, Queen Henrietta Maria had fled to the relative calm of Exeter to give birth to their daughter, Henrietta Anne. After a very difficult birth – there was a strong belief that the Queen might not survive – the newborn baby had been left with Sir John Berkeley in Exeter, while the Queen escaped to France via Falmouth. In July 1644, the King stopped in Exeter to have his first glimpse of his new daughter.

While in Exeter, the King received petitions from many who claimed to have been illegally detained by Sir Richard Grenville; Sir William Courtenay and George Cutteford were amongst the petitioners. Sir William Courtenay, as a staunch Royalist, was probably released immediately, but George Cutteford's petition, along with many others, was initially dismissed.

---

10 Miller, 1979, p. 84.

Cutteford was of no consequence to a King hell-bent on pursuit of the enemy. Only Sir William Courtenay was released, and he returned to the battlefield. His regiment was later sent to Oxford for the defence of the city against besieging Parliamentary forces, while his family's Powderham estate, acting as a Royalist garrison during the war, was decimated by repeated attacks by Parliamentary soldiers. William and his family would not live there again during his lifetime.

In 1645, during the Battle of Bridgwater in Somerset, as Bridgwater Castle was stormed by Parliament's army, Sir William, just seventeen, was wounded in both legs. The Civil War would destroy the fortunes of the Courtenays for many years to come.

Meanwhile, for the remaining months of 1644, George Cutteford remained in Rougemont Castle under guard, and, realising he would probably not survive much longer, he wrote his will.[11] He bequeathed £200 to each of his daughters and the remainder to his eldest son, George Cutteford. They would never receive the money.

Hearing of the arrival of the King in Cornwall, Cornish men now flocked to join the Royalists, and Essex, overwhelmed, was forced to move his men south to Lostwithiel. The castle there provided them with some defence, and they still had the sea behind them, with the possibility of a retreat to Fowey on the coast, but the Royalists planned to starve them out, and effectively cut off their supplies. The sea behind them might have given Essex's army some hope of escape, but a persistent westerly wind prevented Parliament's ships from landing supplies at Fowey or transporting Essex's soldiers safely away.

In desperation, Essex ordered his cavalry – 2,000 men under the command of Sir William Balfour – to make a break through the enemy lines at night. The Royalists failed to prevent their escape, and Balfour's cavalry made it back to Plymouth. It is

---

11 PROB 11/285, a 'proved' copy the will of George Cutteford the younger, dated 13 April 1645, mentions his father's will of July 1644. Held at the National Archives.

not known if Cutteford's sons were among them, but a far worse situation confronted Essex's foot soldiers left behind.

In driving rain, Essex took his infantry along the coast towards Fowey, under constant attack from Grenville's forces. By nightfall, the Parliamentary forces could no longer hold their ground. Suddenly the road to Fowey was blocked, and thousands of men were caught on the coast with no hope of escape.

So Essex deserted them – with Lord Robartes and another officer, the Earl of Essex, so-called commander of the Parliamentary army – and escaped to Plymouth on a fishing boat, leaving his desperate men to face the Royalist forces alone.

Thousands of Essex's men remained; trapped, defeated and compelled to surrender. They received what seemed at first to be generous terms from their attackers. They were set at liberty, providing they left their arms and munitions behind. Unfortunately for them, the local people were not so kind or forgiving – the locals well remembered how Essex's army had stolen food and horses on its way into Cornwall, and now the Cornish people, many Royalist-supporters, wanted their belongings back.

As the unarmed Parliamentary soldiers retreated through Cornwall, they were mercilessly plundered by the Royalist forces and disgruntled civilians, taking their clothes, their boots, any money and food, leaving them with little to survive the long walk back to Devon. Many died of exposure along the way or were murdered simply for their boots. It is said that of the 6,000 men walking home from Cornwall, only 1,000 made it back, though this obviously takes no account of deserters, and, after the behaviour of Essex and Robartes, there were sure to be many running away.

The King was delighted with this victory at Lostwithiel, though he expressed concern at the treatment of the enemy forces. King Charles granted Sir Richard Grenville further lands in Devon, including Buckland Abbey, a large manor with extensive grounds, just north of Plymouth. Buckland

Abbey had been built by Sir Richard's grandfather and name-
sake, hero of the *Revenge*. Years before, the famous privateer
Sir Francis Drake had put in a bid for the Buckland estate,
but the elder Sir Richard Grenville was not on good terms
with Drake, and had instead sold the manor to Sir Christopher
Harris of Radford Park. But Drake had schemed with Sir
Christopher over the deal, and, after paying Grenville senior,
Sir Christopher subsequently handed Buckland Abbey over to
Sir Francis Drake for a small fee. The Grenville family were still
embittered by the subterfuge, but now, at last, in September
1644, the King returned the house to its 'rightful owner', Sir
Richard Grenville.

But of course, Sir Francis Drake the privateer was long dead,
and the house had come into the hands of the Courtenays by
marriage.[12] The young Sir William Courtenay must have been
horrified to hear of the loss of even more of his property, particularly to a man who was supposedly an ally. Sir William was
probably then in Oxford, and complained about the matter
to the King's Lord Chamberlain there, George Cutteford's old
friend, the Earl of Dorset.

Sir Richard Grenville was making enemies on both sides
of the war, but was oblivious to any complaints. By the
time he returned to reinstate the siege on Plymouth, Sir
Richard owned Buckland Abbey, all the estates of his wife
Mary Howard, and all the Devon properties of the Earl of
Bedford. Also, during the Lostwithiel campaign, Sir Richard
had taken the opportunity to seize Lord Robartes' house,
Lanhdyrock, north of Lostwithiel, and had removed £2,000
worth of valuables.

For the first time in his life, Sir Richard was truly a wealthy
landowner. Only Walreddon was not in his possession, but if he
could capture Cutteford's sons and find the lease, Grenville was
sure he would soon have the full set. Why Richard Grenville

---

12 After the death of his first wife, the elder Sir William Courtney married
    Elizabeth Sydenham, widow of Sir Francis Drake, who retained an interest in
    the Buckland Abbey estates.

didn't just kill George Cutteford, and take all his estates by force, is a puzzle left to history. Grenville seemed determined to have Walreddon back by legal means, and wanted Cutteford alive to witness his own defeat. However, George Cutteford hadn't lost the battle yet, and, unknown to Grenville, his allies were marshalling some secret forces that would defeat Grenville and have Cutteford released.

On 5 September 1644, Grenville joined the King gathering an army in Tavistock to attempt another attack on Plymouth. The garrison was in a desperate state: 2,000 of their men had been lost at Lostwithiel, leaving only 800 to defend a line of over 4 miles, against a Royalist force of over 10,000. There was a serious shortage of arms and ammunition, but still the towns-people refused to accept the King's call to surrender. Instead, the trumpeter who brought the request from the King was beaten, imprisoned and sent back to the Royalist camp with a warning that he would be hanged if he returned to Plymouth.

The King established his headquarters at Widey Court, overlooking Plymouth's fortifications from the north. Around him, the lands of the Trelawneys, including their Ham House estates, had been obliterated by Parliament. Robert Trelawney, a relative of George Halse's guardian, Francis Trelawney, had been captured by Parliament, and died in prison in London in 1644. The Trelawneys were another family whose fortunes were destroyed by Civil War. At nearby Widey Court, overlooking country cleared for battle and laid waste by war, the King formulated his plans of attack. He intended that Plymouth should fall.

In the end, the King's attack on Plymouth did not last long. There were skirmishes between the opposing forces, and the King set up cannon along a ridge that the Plymouth people would derisively call 'vapouring hill' (now called Vapron) where the cannon let off a great deal of smoke, but the shots seemed to miss their targets. The Puritan population of Plymouth saw their successful defence of the town, against such insurmountable odds, as deliverance by God.

Instead of ordering a full attack, the King suddenly withdrew his forces and took his army to Exeter. Having travelled so far through Cornwall in terrible weather, his troops were probably crippled by disease and fatigue, unready for another major assault, and the King saw other battles in need of reinforcements in the east. He left Grenville in charge of the Plymouth blockade, Grenville boasting to his departing monarch how he would take the town by Christmas. But Plymouth would bring him tragedy, not triumph.

Chapter Nine

A Fool and His Money

In September 1644, an officer called Joseph Grenville appeared in the Plymouth garrison, having, he claimed, deserted the Royalists to take up arms with Parliament. He was thought to be Sir Richard's illegitimate son, born in 1628, and now sixteen. One Parliamentary paper called him a 'whelp of Skellum Grenville'.[1] It may seem strange that a boy so young was well received, but the garrison was desperate for all the fighters they could recruit, and reinforcements from London were getting younger all the time. Running out of men, London had recently sent them a shipload of apprentices,

Southgate, Exeter, from Britton's *Beauties of England and Wales*.

---

1   Miller, 1979, p. 94.

boys of twelve; their muskets like tree trunks propped beside
them. If a boy survived to be fourteen, it was quite likely he
would be made a captain, leading his young charges into battle.
The attrition of war made children into seasoned warriors.

Joseph Grenville had an ulterior motive, however. The
troops inside Plymouth garrison, he'd heard, were disgruntled and discontented and, with sufficient financial incentives,
might be persuaded to betray their posts. Hearing one officer,
a Colonel Searle, complaining bitterly of the long nights and
drawn-out engagements, Joseph offered him £3,000 if he
would give up the outworks to the Royalists. But Searle was
still a loyal officer and Joseph Grenville was seized and questioned by Lord Robartes. To his honour, the young Joseph
Grenville admitted and revealed nothing, even when threatened with execution.

His father sent a messenger to Robartes to offer terms
for the boy's life – but of course, Robartes was unmoved.
Robartes own young family were prisoners of the Royalists,
and his lands at Lanhydrock had been sequestered by Richard
Grenville, so he was unlikely to feel any sympathy for the dis-
traught man. Joseph Grenville was taken in chains to Mount
Gould, a high ground on the edge of Plymouth, in full view of
Sir Richard and his forces, and hanged as a traitor.

Sir Richard tried once more to destroy the town with subterfuge, paying some informers within the garrison to set fire
to the town in three places. He hoped to distract Robartes's
soldiers so that he might make a successful attack from the
north. The plan failed. Robartes, hearing of the strategy, held
his men in check, permitting Grenville and his forces to come
within pistol shot of the fortifications before they opened fire
and killed many of Grenville's men.

In October, Robartes made a successful sally across the
mouth of the Tamar River, to capture the town of Saltash.
From there, the men of the Plymouth garrison would have an
excellent strategic position not only to counter future attacks
by Grenville, but to make their way back into Cornwall.

Grenville immediately assembled his forces, blockaded Saltash and after a fierce battle over three days, drove out the Plymouth soldiers, forcing their retreat down a steep slope into the darkness and into the Tamar River. For Robartes' cavalry, in particular, the treacherous descent into the river must have been a terrifying ordeal, with men and horses losing their lives in the escape.

It was a notable victory for Grenville, and he was determined to show no mercy to the captured enemy. He set about hanging 300 of them. Of course, Grenville wanted revenge for the death of his son, Joseph, and he was sick of the continuing failure of his own attempts at taking Plymouth. The prisoners at Saltash provided him with the ready means of expressing his rage. The King, hearing of the intended massacre, sent orders for the prisoners' lives to be spared, but Grenville disobeyed him. Many prisoners were hanged regardless.

This was a dangerous development in what was proving, much to the King's disgust, to be a very ungentlemanly war. Of course, he had heard the rumours of Grenville's behaviour at Lydford, and had requested that the hangings there be stopped, but until now he had not the time, nor the motive, to address the matter. Now he did. There were also rumours that Grenville, now Sheriff of Devon, was embezzling substantial sums from the war funds. Building materials intended for huts for soldiers were instead used to construct a fine riding stables at Buckland Abbey, for Grenville's personal use. Contributions from landowners that were supposed to go to the King were suddenly in Grenville's pockets. If he wasn't paid, Grenville would issue a warrant for the debtor's arrest. If the constables refused to issue the warrants, Grenville had them hanged.

The King's officials in Oxford, including the Earl of Dorset, were expressing deep concerns about Grenville's finances. Grenville's solders were well disciplined and were renowned for not stealing from the local population – in contrast to many soldiers who, in desperation, were forced to take whatever they could get from the local population, and so were living on plunder. But Grenville himself was the ultimate thief. When Tavistock's millers, who supported Parliament, refused to mill corn for his soldiers, Grenville had them all hanged; the King's subjects were at the mercy of a madman.

The Earl of Dorset had possibly been warning King Charles of Grenville's dangerous personality for some time, but it was only now that the King realised he needed to do something to curb the brutality of Grenville's rule and bring his errant general back into line – without of course admitting that Grenville's appointment had been a mistake.

As the King's forces made their way towards Oxford, some-one – just who will be revealed later – brought the petition of George Cutteford to the King's attention. Here was a case that might just teach Grenville a lesson, without causing a major scandal, and punish him sufficiently to force him back into serving the King and not his own fortunes.

King Charles granted Cutteford a hearing, and requested that Sir John Berkeley, Governor of Exeter, review the case with some urgency. Berkeley was no friend of Grenville's, jeal-ous of Grenville's success and wary of Grenville's methods. He was more than happy to take up the petition, and to become part of a Commission that the King established to investigate Sir Richard Grenville's actions in Devon.

It may seem that the significance of this development is exaggerated, but the timing is remarkable. The King had received petitions from many prisoners and their fami-lies over many months, many complaining of Sir Richard Grenville's actions. Cutteford's petition was just another in the pile. For a man of George Cutteford's background, a Puritan with no allegiance to the Royalist cause, to be granted not only the possibility of release but an investiga-tion into his circumstances, an investigation that would at least embarrass if not undermine one of the most prominent and successful Royalist Generals of the English Civil War – Cutteford himself must have thought this was nothing short of a miracle.

For the first time in many months, George had a hope of release. However, in an act of sheer audacity, Cutteford wrote to thank the King for the hearing, and request that he be released immediately so he might gather his papers to support the case.[2] This second petition is one of the rare surviving documents that describe George Cutteford's situation, and it is an illuminating read. For a man in such desperate circumstances, probably made ill and wretched by his privations, the logic and daring of his arguments is remarkable. There is brilliance in his boldness.

For the petition is a beautifully worded series of lies.

His petition opens with a plea for his Majesty to protect George Cutteford's son from attack by Richard Grenville. It seems that Grenville was actively searching for the young man, hoping to imprison him too, in his search for the lease. However, Cutteford makes no mention that his son is in fact fighting against the King, and with Parliament's forces.

He continues with a requests for release from Rougemont, so he might fetch his papers for the hearing with the King's Commissioners in Exeter, already there investigating Grenville's financial misdealings. Cutteford explains that the papers were hidden while Essex's forces were in Tavistock – though of course they had been hidden from Royalist Sir Richard well before that. Sir John Berkeley adds his own coda to the petition, requesting permission from King Charles to pass the petition and other documents to the King's Commissioners. The King responded with notes on the reverse, advising Berkeley and the Commissioners to consider what Cutteford owed to Richard Grenville and what payments Cutteford may have made to Mary Howard and her family. King Charles had also received a petition from Mary Howard and her son, George Howard, with details of the money Cutteford had sent to them as their employee. The tragedy of the petition from George Cutteford is revealed in close study of the hand-writing. The added note

---

2 Add Ms 18008-818, 1644. Held at West Sussex Record Office.

from Berkeley and the petition itself are written in the same handwriting, both parts probably written by Sir John Berkeley himself. It seems that George Cutteford, this man of papers, was already too ill after his long imprisonment to write in his own defence.

On 6 November 1644, George Cutteford was given a hearing by the King's commissioners, including Sir John Berkeley. They considered his case, and the accounts, as described by Mary Howard, of how he had supported her and her children for over ten years.

Richard Grenville, still attacking Plymouth, was not present, but he charged Cutteford with having sent Mary Howard money to fund Parliament's army. This was not untrue, as Mary had paid for the younger George Cutteford's commission in Drake's regiment, and she was also probably supporting her nephew, now the Earl of Suffolk, a leader in the Parliamentary forces.

The Commissioners deliberated, and the outcome was not entirely in George Cutteford's favour; it certainly would have riled Sir Richard Grenville, however. The Commissioners directed Sir Richard to restore Walreddon to the Cuttefords, along with all the corn and livestock he had stolen from the property. In return, George Cutteford was required to pay Sir Richard all the rent from Walreddon and Mary's other properties, since November 1641, deducting any and all sums paid to Mary Howard and her children over the same period. Considering the condition of the estates, and the amounts that must have been sent to Mary Howard over the years, the resulting balance was not to amount to very much at all.

The strangest decision concerned George Howard. Mary Vernon and George Howard had both been receiving regular payments from Cutteford. Since Mary had lost all her property, and was no longer able to provide for her children, Sir Richard Grenville was now required to provide them with an allowance.

Sir Richard must have been furious. Not only was Walreddon back in Cutteford's hands, with little money in compensation, but suddenly he was forced to outlay even more money to the daughter of Charles Howard, Mary Vernon. And even worse, he was now responsible for the upkeep, education and outstanding wardship payments for a step-son and heir he didn't know existed – to some boy he'd never even heard of before, who was rumoured to be Mary's illegitimate son. Who was this George Howard? If he was by law the son of Charles Howard, and now his step-son, this George Howard had a right to at least a sizeable share of everything Richard Grenville owned.

Here was the King's trump card. Grenville may have thought he had, at last, amassed a personal fortune, worthy of his new-found status, but discovered that the King could give it away, even to the sons of his enemies. Enraged, and realising his position was more precarious that he thought, Grenville decided to make a full attack on Plymouth. Perhaps he had even received word that George Cutteford's family was in Plymouth. He could not have chosen a worse moment to attack.

On 8 January 1645, Grenville amassed a considerable body of cavalry and infantry, over 6,000 men, and hurled them against the town. He anticipated at least annihilation, if not extermination. He expected to have taken Plymouth by morning. He demanded nothing less than a complete victory over his enemies.

But it rained. Not just a little rain, not a light shower, but a torrent that drove them back. It rained for two days. With the ditches before the line of earthworks filled with water, there was no chance of Grenville's men even reaching the walls. Men and horses were flailing, drowning in the mud. But Sir Richard kept sending them. Again and again, he ordered his forces forward, to attack the fortifications. He blamed his subordinates, not the weather, for their failure to take Plymouth. On the night of the 10 January, he tried again, this time with some success. The Royalist cannon thundered through the night, and he managed to take two of the forts – but only briefly before being driven back. Sixty of his men were killed at Maudlyn. It was said that one of the Plymouth captains managed to turn a cannon on the enemy and killed thirty with one shot, the night air filled with the screams and cries of dying Royalists.

Grenville managed to hold the fort at Little PennyComequick for a bit longer, but silence gave them away. An officer called Birch, having fought amongst the screams and shouts at Maudlyn, noticed that the fort at Little Pennycomequick was quiet – too quiet. He ordered his men to approach in the darkness. Hearing someone within cry out, 'Stand, who are you for?'[3] Birch replied 'For the Parliament!' – and the subsequent rain of gunfire upon them told them the fort had been taken by Grenville's men. Birch's men bravely charged the fort and took it back, killing or capturing a further sixty-six of Grenville's men.

Sir Richard ordered yet another attack on Plymouth's defences, but one of his officers, Colonel Champernowne, protested, declaring that Grenville's rash behaviour had caused the failure of the previous attacks. Sir Richard called him a coward, at which Champernowne fired his pistol at Grenville, but to no effect. Sir Richard then fired his own pistol at Champernowne and killed the man. When the Colonel's brother retaliated with pistol-fire of his own, Grenville drew his sword and ran him through.

Again Sir Richard attacked Plymouth, this time occupying Mount Stamford to the east of the harbour, and again the garrison beat him back. Sir Richard Grenville would never manage to take Plymouth, however many of his own men he killed in the attempt.

By March 1645, the King was losing the war. Parliament had successfully restructured its forces and the New Model Army was born, eventually commanded by their most famous General, Oliver Cromwell. Cromwell's forces were eager to take the west.

---

3   Miller, 1979, p. 100.

The King and his councillors proposed to counter this with the formation of the Western Association, combining the remaining forces of Cornwall, Devon, Somerset and Dorset, with the King's young son Charles overseeing the Western armies. The aim was to unite all of the King's supporters, quell the animosities between the bickering leaders, and so unify the Royalist cause into stronger, combined attacks.

Prince Charles, just fifteen, was still impressed by Grenville's victories, despite the doubts of his father. He summoned Grenville to bring his forces to join the King's army, under General Goring, to assist in the capture of Taunton, north-east of Exeter. Grenville ignored the summons. Prince Charles and his counsellors summoned him again. Grenville ignored the summons again, and only after repeated requests did he reluctantly bring a force of 3,000 with him to Taunton. He left 2,000 men still blockading Plymouth. His belligerent reluctance to fight with the King's re-structured army would result in his final downfall.

In early April 1645, Grenville set about reducing Taunton, as ordered. He began the attack in his usual manner, by kidnapping an old man called Syms, a local justice of the peace, and demanding Mr Syms pay him a £1,000 within three days. While waiting for his money, Sir Richard established his men within musket shot of the town, and delayed the attack while he went to survey Wellington House, a Parliamentary stronghold 5 miles west of Taunton. They promptly shot him.

It seems Grenville got too close while inspecting the enemy stronghold, and one of their bullets struck Richard Grenville in the thigh. The wound was so serious that, for a while, it was thought it would kill him. The Parliamentary newsletters were ecstatic, some wrongly reporting his death, while others describing how the bullets had blasted his groin – just desserts for a 'noteable whoremaster'.[4] But news of his death and injuries

---

4   Miller, 1979, p. 25.

were exaggerated. Instead, Sir John Berkeley was summoned to take command of his forces, while Sir Richard was, to some embarrassment, carted off in a litter, and transported to Exeter.

Sir John was rightly concerned that Grenville's men, fiercely loyal to their leader, particularly as he paid them so much, would not obey him. As Grenville lay wounded, the Prince's Commissioners sought to have Grenville's reassurances that his men would obey Berkeley, but as Grenville was carried away on the litter, they noticed Sir Richard giving whispered instructions to his officers. Sure enough, Grenville's officers and men refused to serve Berkeley. In fact, when Sir John Berkeley ordered one of Grenville's men, a Lieutenant-Colonel Thomas Robinson, not to burn down Wellington House, Robinson rode directly to his true master, Sir Richard Grenville, recovering in Exeter, for further orders. Robinson returned and Wellington House was duly burned to the ground, directly contravening Berkeley's orders.

Sir John Berkeley did manage to spare Mr Syms from paying the £1,000 ransom to Grenville. Sir John wrote a nice note, explaining that it seemed unfair to be demanding money from an aged and respectable man such as Mr Syms. Grenville was furious, believing that Berkeley had robbed him. He sent a written reply 'so full of ill language and reproach'[5] that his allies were appalled. Sir Richard complained about Berkeley to the Prince's Council.

To make matters worse for Grenville, he discovered that his old enemy George Cutteford was still alive and living in Exeter as a free man. Cutteford had been released by the King's Commissioners in December, but had been very ill, probably too ill to travel far in winter. While recovering, and trying to arrange his affairs to meet the demands of the King's Commissioners, it is very likely that George Cutteford had

---

5   The story of the blackmailing of Mr Syms is told on p. 126 of Granville, R, 1908, *The King's General in the West; the Life of Sir Richard Granville*, Bart., 1600–1659, originally published by J. Lane of London. Sadly, the only copy I can obtain is a poorly reproduced print copy published by www.general-books. net, though their digital version is very good.

remained in Exeter. Cutteford had also thought with good reason that, while Grenville was blockading Plymouth and then Taunton, Exeter was the safest place for him to stay.

After so many months of incarceration, Cutteford's freedom was sadly short-lived. By a tragic turn of events, in mid-April 1644, Sir Richard Grenville arrived unexpectedly in Exeter, borne on a litter, wounded, to discover his old enemy living close by. There was now no reason for Grenville to keep Cutteford alive. On 16 April 1644, probably at the hands of Richard Grenville and men hired for the purpose, George Cutteford was dead.

Chapter Ten

A Man of Means

On 13 April 1646, just a few days short of the anniversary of his father's death, George Cutteford the younger entered Exeter with Parliament's army. Sir John Berkeley had at last surrendered the city to Parliament, his Royalist forces fleeing after a lengthy and horrendous siege, and George arrived in a city devastated by war and overwhelmed by starving refugees. The Parliamentary army looted whatever they could find and the more 'godly' amongst them set about destroying church buildings.

In the midst of this chaos, George's first task was to find an attorney and make his will. Perhaps he wrote the will himself, as the original document is missing and only the version

Charles II. (Courtesy of the Library of Congress, Prints & Photographs Division, LC-USZ62-38492)

'proved' in Canterbury in 1658 remains.[1] George gave money to the poor of Whitchurch and to a dozen of his servants, £10 to his lawyer William Harris of Tavistock, £10 to his nephew and godson George Donne, and another £10 to his aunt, Joan Donne.[2] His kinsman Philip Halse received £20, and his part of the estate of Gawton in Tavistock; £50 was bequeathed to each of his sister's sons, George and Robert Radford – it seems that Grace Cutteford, the younger, had married into the Radford family, though she would marry again in the 1650s.[3]

The sum of £200 had been allocated to each of his sisters in his father's will, but the money had never been paid, and George Cutteford the younger had insufficient funds to pay it now. So he gave his sister Grace his home called Woodford, in Whitchurch, in lieu of her father's money, and a further £100. To his sister Anne, he bestowed his farm called Tuddy Brooke, again in lieu of the money, and a £100. His sister Eleanor had died in 1644, but the money from their father's will was still owing to her husband John Skerrit, so George bequeathed John Skerrit two small estates he owned in Whitchurch: his house and lands called Ponniton, then occupied by Edmund and John Drake; and his small estate called Bamton, its tenants John and Richard Chubb. He also refunded John Skerrit the £90 John had paid to satisfy the late George Cutteford's outstanding debts, and £10 went to each of John Skerrit's children.

Thomas Robinson also received £10, which seems strange if this is indeed the same Thomas Robinson who worked for

---

1 PROB 11/285, a copy of the will of George Cutteford the younger, dated 13 April 1646, and 'proved' at Canterbury in 1658; held at the National Archives, London. During the Interregnum, Cromwell had many administrative functions 'centralised' and subsequently all wills had to be 'proved' or processed in Canterbury.

2 From document PROB 11/285, dated 1658, held at the National Archives, London. George Cutteford bequeaths money to his aunt, Joan Donne, who I presume was his father George Cutteford's sister.

3 Add Ms 18008-826, undated, but circa 1660. Held at West Sussex Record Office. These detailed accounts of John Cutteford describe his sister as Grace Gyhonville. Though the surname is difficult to decipher, it still suggests she re-married.

Richard Grenville and caused so much grief to his father. Perhaps George Cutteford the younger was ignorant of Tom Robinson's history.

To his mother, Grace Cutteford, George bequeathed £100 and the remainder of his estate – the grand manor and grounds of Walreddon and the surrounding cottages and farms, including two mills. His brother John was named executor of the will.

It was a very different will to his grandfather's in 1582: £400 was all William Cutteford the sailor had to offer. Now his grandson George Cutteford owned most of Whitchurch, some very fine houses and was bequeathing away nearly £1,000, but he did not live to enjoy it. Within five days, before 18 April 1646, George Cutteford the younger was dead too.[4] When the younger George Cutteford wrote his will, he knew he didn't have long to live. He was probably badly wounded in the battle to re-take Exeter and hurried to make his last will and testament, to provide for his family. George Cutteford, father and son, did not live to see the end of the war.

George Howard, the son of Mary Howard and George Cutteford, faired a great deal better. At the end of the war, in 1646[5], in the midst of the chaos and the homeless and the grieving, he inherited all his mother's estates – 4,000 acres in four counties, over thirty properties including Fitzford. He still owned the Clun Castle estates in Shropshire, from his 'father', Charles Howard.

Lanhydrock, stolen by Richard Grenville, was returned by Parliament to Lord Robartes, but, in a strange turn of events, Buckland Abbey and the lands around neighbouring Buckland Monachorum were not returned to the Courtenays. Parliament sequestered many properties once belonging to their Royalist

---

4 Radford, 1890, describes George Cutteford the younger's burial in
    Whitchurch on 18 April 1646.

5 1646 was the end of the 'First Civil War'. The conflict between Parliament
    and the King's supporters continued for many years, with the final battle of
    the 'Second Civil War' on 3 September 1651 at Worcester. (www.british-civil-
    wars.co.uk)

enemies, and it seems the Buckland estates were awarded to George Howard.[6] He certainly received property in nearby Buckland Monachorum. As the (apparent) cousin of James Howard, Earl of Suffolk, who had fought for Parliament, George Howard proved his allegiance to Parliament with ease. Concealing his true parentage was very much to his advantage.[7]

In London in 1649, Oliver Cromwell and his Parliament tried and beheaded King Charles I. Just a few months later, George Howard returned to Fitzford with his mother, to find the house almost destroyed by the Earl of Essex's forces. Cash for rebuilding was in short supply, so George Howard arranged a loan from Henry Rexford in Plymouth. From Rexford's surviving correspondence, it seems he was in the business of making substantial loans to many of the gentry, now impoverished by the war. Rexford was one of the few businessmen who prospered in Plymouth during the siege, probably making his fortune from shipping.

Rexford's clients were always very pleasant in their requests to delay re-payments, frequently pleading, almost obsequious in their letters.[8] In 1651, George Howard too wrote to Rexford to explain he would be paying his first instalments once he had received the full account details of the loan. The note is short and straightforward, less sycophantic that most, and written on notepaper with the watermark of the Howard symbol: a Tudor rose.

In this new world, unsteadily forging a new constitution without a head of state, this was a dangerous act. Although his cousins the Howards had fought for Parliament, they had changed sides in 1646, supporting the King's sons in prison

---

6   Document D1508M/Moger/396, dated 1663, held at Devon Record Office, is just one of a number of documents describing land deals between George Howard and various tenants at Buckland Monachorum.

7   James Howard, Earl of Suffolk, may have fought for Parliament during the English Civil War, but in 1647, he was imprisoned by Parliament for being a suspected Royalist. See Jeffrey, 1997.

8   Documents 1/642/67, dated 1639-1653, held at Plymouth and West Devon Record Office, include this letter from George Howard to Henry Rexford.

and in exile in France.[9] Of all the surnames George could
choose – Halse, Cutteford, even Royalist names like Trelawney
or Grenville – to proclaim himself a Howard during the reign
of Cromwell was a poor decision, and he must have been
forced to live very quietly in Devon for fear of imprisonment
himself. Of course, George Howard lived a comfortable life.
He was arguably the richest man in Devon. The sailor William
Cutteford would have been astonished by his grandson's
wealth and status.

During the 1650s, George Howard and his mother set about
repairing and redecorating Fitzford, which was restored to
its former splendour. Mary brought her furniture, books and
other belongings from her house in London and never seems
to have returned there, settling in Fitzford for the remainder of
her life. The decor was luxurious even for the time, with the
furnishings of the 'best bed chamber'[10] worth three times as
much as that in the parlour. Mrs Radford in 1890[11] describes
the extensive refurbishment: the blue bedroom; the green bedroom; the 'half-moon' chamber; Mr Howard's bedroom; and
Mary Howard's chamber, with the bed perfumed; lavish dress-
ing rooms and servants' quarters; and a valuable library. The
house resumed the bustling activities of a great estate, brewing
beer and cider, salting meat, and storing plentiful food for the
winter months.

The money for all this restoration was raised on rents from
tenants who had suffered greatly during the war, often at the
hands of Mary Howard's husband. Many of the original tenants

---

9 George Howard's cousin and namesake, Hon. George Howard, brother of
   the Earl of Suffolk, fought for Parliament during the war, but then changed
   sides. In 1647, the Hon. George Howard became Master of the Horse to
   King Charles I's second son James, Duke of York. Hon. George Howard then
   worked as a close adviser to the Duke, as Gentleman of the Bedchamber,
   while the Duke was under house arrest by Parliament. With the Earl of
   Suffolk and his uncle, Sir William Howard, imprisoned for being Royalists,
   and Hon. George Howard now imprisoned with the King's son, it seems the
   Interregnum was bent on destroying the fortunes of the Howard family.

10 Radford, 1890, p. 99.

11 Radford, 1890, p. 99.

were dead, some of them imprisoned and killed at Lydford by Grenville's men. The Devon countryside was now populated by thousands of impoverished and grieving widows and children. Much of their cattle and corn – and even furniture – had been stolen by Grenville's soldiers. But Mary Howard and her son continued to collect the rent, to fund the redecoration of Fitzford.

Meanwhile, the deaths of George Cutteford the elder and the younger left a family in deepest mourning. Grace Cutteford, now a grieving mother and widow, returned to Walreddon, her daughters and grandchildren living around her in Whitchurch. But times were hard, and Grace was determined to recover everything her husband had once claimed as his own. Therefore, Grace wrote to Mary Howard requesting her husband's income from Okehampton Park, but Mary was officious and cold in her reply[12], explaining that she had transferred the income from Okehampton Park to George Cutteford, in lieu of wages, for his lifetime only. There had, she explained, never been any suggestion that the Cuttefords should have access to that income after George Cutteford's death. Mary curtly ended the letter, 'And [I] shall ever be as much your friend as you give me cause'.[13] Grace Cutteford was a bitter woman, with just cause – her husband had been killed by Mary Howard's husband, after all – so she took Mary Howard to court.

The battle between the two women went on and on, Grace refusing to give up the matter, Mary refusing to give in. Relations between the two women had never been friendly, understandably. The court costs escalated, until Grace Cutteford could no longer afford to pay the rent on Walreddon and she was forced to leave the estate. George Howard bought the lease for Walreddon and its farms for just £300.[14] After George Cutteford had spent so many months in prison, battling Grenville over the lease for

---

12 Radford, 1890, p. 100.

13 Radford, 1890, p. 100.

14 D1508M/Moger/434 dated 1665, and held at Devon Record Office.

the sake of his family's future, George Howard's payment to his father's family seems a paltry sum.

What happened to Grace Cutteford's daughters isn't known, though Anne Robinson, then a widow, took her brother's will to Canterbury to be proved in 1658, so she must have kept Tuddy Brooke farm. Her brother John should have dealt with the matter, as executor of the will, but he had found employment in Bristol as a 'wayter and searcher'[15], his father's old friend John Maynard giving him a reference.[16] After a childhood of lofty aspirations, John Cutteford was forced to return to his father's old trade as a customs officer.

John and his mother fell out over the finances, and John refused to talk to her again. Grace Cutteford moved to St Thomas in Exeter, living on charity for the rest of her life. The area around St Thomas had been flattened during the siege of Exeter, to deny any cover to potential attackers, and was now being hurriedly re-built to house the thousands of homeless, including Grace. It was a sorry end to everything George Cutteford the elder had dreamed of for his family.

His son George Howard did try to do his bit to improve the world. He gave money to charity, and he was kind to the Puritan minister, Thomas Larkham, appointed by the people of Tavistock.[17] And he had his own tragedies to bear. In 1655, Howard married a local woman called Mary Burnby, and they lived at Hayes End in Tamerton Foliot, but his wife died in childbirth, and the child, baptised George, did not live long; he died in 1658. Suddenly there was no one to inherit the Fitz estates, for George Howard never re-married (which was very unusual for the time).

---

15 Add Ms 18008, John Cutteford's papers, held at West Sussex Record Office. Also see the website for the University of Exeter's Centre for Historical Maritime Studies: http://centres.exeter.ac.uk/cmhs

16 Add Ms 18008-826 undated but circa 1660, held at West Sussex Record Office, mentions John Maynard, most likely the future Sir John Maynard, giving John Cutteford a reference for the job of customs officer (though John Cutteford, it seems, had to pay for it!).

17 Woodcock, 2008. Also see Alford, 1891, and Radford, 1890, pp. 98, 99 and 103.

In 1660, after the death of Oliver Cromwell, the monarchy was restored and the son of the executed King Charles I was crowned King Charles II. George Howard then threw all his energies into politics. He and his father's old friend Sir John Maynard were returned as members of the newly constituted Parliament, representing Bere Alston, though George Howard eventually chose to represent Tavistock with his uncle Sir William Russell.[18]

Russell and George Howard were both Whigs, a faction of Parliament urgently trying, and failing, to curb the powers of the new King. Of course, George Howard could be an MP, with a say in the new constitution, only because he was a landowner – he owed all his success and status to the efforts of his unacknowledged father. In fact, George the younger had been instrumental in getting his father released from prison all those years ago. How did George Cutteford, just one of so many prisoners at Lydford and then Exeter, get the attention of the King? The key to the success of his son's petition lies in a group of men on both sides of the Civil War, a shadowy group that possibly included George Howard; a group of conspirators in the 1640s, who were battling for peace.

Like a chess board, where a knot of black and white pieces are in heated discussions on one side of the board, as the pawns are being massacred around them, the English Civil War had split the country, but not everything was black versus white. Some of the combatants, all moderates in their political and religious views, were desperately trying to change the nature of game, conspiring amidst the skirmishes and bloodshed for an end to the war. And all of these men, on both sides of the conflict, were friends of George Cutteford, relations of Mary Howard, and sworn enemies of Richard Grenville.

---

18 George Howard was returned as a Member of Parliament for two constituencies in 1660: for Bere Alston, with Sir John Maynard, and for Tavistock, with Sir William Russell. George Howard chose to represent Tavistock, and another representative for Bere Alston was appointed.

The first of these was Sir John Maynard, an old family friend to the Cuttefords. He had had great success in his life, as an attorney to King Charles I, but when war was declared he sided with Parliament. The ensuing war, however, dismayed him – not because of the thousands slain, but because the war was costing the country, and him, a fortune.[19] Like his friends the Earl of Essex and Bulstrode Whitelaw, Maynard was very worried about the costs of the war, and also about the rising military power of Oliver Cromwell, the Parliamentary General. In 1644, John Maynard secretly met with the Earl of Essex – and others – in an effort to have Cromwell indicted. Cromwell's plans for a New Model Army, the first professional army in England, made them uneasy, and they were concerned that in the distractions of the Civil War, in the midst of the fighting over religious, financial and political differences, there would be a military coup. They were right to be concerned – in 1646, Cromwell and his New Model Army did invade London and take over the Government, and in 1649 they beheaded the King. Cromwell subsequently reigned over Britain and Ireland as a military dictator.

In 1644, as George Cutteford suffered in gaol, John Maynard and his friends could see the future; they knew they had to end the war, by any means necessary. At the moment that George Cutteford's case was finally being heard, in November 1644, Cutteford's old friend John Maynard was visiting the King in Oxford, negotiating peace.

THE MAYNARDS

The Maynard family have had a long history in Devon. In 1569, three sons – John, Oliver and Nicholas Maynard – presented themselves for the compulsory muster roll in Milton

---

19 See Alford, 1891, who describes in scathing terms Sir John Maynard's notorious avarice. Sir John, it seems, was not a man generally liked or trusted.

Abbot, a parish belonging to the 'Tavistock Hundred', an administrative region of 100 parishes around and about the town of Tavistock.[20] Milton Abbot is located north west of Tavistock, mid-way between Tavistock and Launceston.

The three sons were probably farmers. Unlike sons of the wealthy, they were not required to provide supplies of weapons, armour or horses, though they were required to maintain their personal weaponry and armour.

In the 1560s, the Spanish armies were gathering in Holland and appeared to be a threat. By 1569, compulsory musters were a regular event throughout the country, and the three sons duly attended the muster at Milton Abbot. Nicholas was a pikeman, wearing light body armour and wielding a pikestaff. Oliver was an archer, carrying a long bow and a sheaf of twenty-four arrows. John Maynard was a harquebusier; he deployed a harquebus firearm, an early form of musket about 3ft long, weighing about 10 pounds and fired by lighting the pan of powder with a lighted wick.

It is not known whether the three sons ever did fight in battle, but their many descendants would become influential and wealthy people throughout Devon. All Presbyterians and committed to their faith, their wealth would be used to establish schools and almshouses in Tavistock, Exeter and Plymouth. In 1602, Oliver Maynard, the archer, established 'The Gift House', an almshouse once in Tavistock, on Barley Market Street, housing twelve people: four couples and four widows. 'The Gift House', later known as 'Maynard's House', remained there as a charitable institution until the mid-1800s.[21]

John Maynard, the harquebusier, had three sons: John, Alexander and Thomas. John Maynard the younger established himself in Plymouth, and became a very wealthy

20 See the Muster Roll for Milton Abbot in 1569, transcribed by Philippa Stout, at www.devonheritage.org.uk

21 See White's Devonshire Directory of 1850 which describes the 'Gift House' at Tavistock.

merchant and attorney, building almshouses and schools in Plymouth and Exeter. He was one of the first to provide funds for a school for the education of women, known as Maynard's School, which is still in Exeter. It was the third school for girls ever built in Britain. It was John Maynard the younger who witnessed the will of his friend, the sailor William Cutteford, and probably supervised the education of William's son George.[22]

Alexander Maynard, his brother, established himself as an attorney in Tavistock, probably working for the Stannary Court. It is said he lived at Abbey House in Tavistock, though the building later known as the Abbey House, located on the grounds of the former Abbey (where the Bedford Hotel is today), was not developed as a residence until about 1720. Alexander Maynard married Honora Arscott and they had four sons, the second son, John, born in 1602, achieving great renown as Sir John Maynard, lawyer and politician. Alexander's son, the future Sir John Maynard, attended Exeter College, Oxford in 1618, at just sixteen years old, and entered the Middle Temple in 1619. In 1640, he was appointed as Recorder for Plymouth, the highest legal position in Plymouth, and became the representative for Totnes in Parliament. There he advocated the end to feudal wardships, which would eventually result in the dissolution of the Court of Wards.

In the build-up to the English Civil War, Sir John supported Parliament, worried about King Charles I's religious views, but more importantly Charles's denial that the rules of *habeas corpus* could not be applied to the monarch. King Charles felt he could imprison anyone who opposed him, without trial or account. During the ensuing Civil War, Maynard's Tavistock home was ransacked and nearly destroyed by Royalists. Staying in London, Sir John was

---

22 There are many John Maynards in the history of Devon. I have pieced together the family relationships as best as I can from existing records, but I cannot guarantee that I have always found the correct John Maynard.

worried by the rising military power of Oliver Cromwell and joined with the Earl of Essex, Bulstrode Whitlocke and other Parliamentary supporters in an anti-Cromwellian faction, attempting to take action against Cromwell as an incendiary, but it came to nothing.

In November 1644, John Maynard and his colleague Bulstrode Whitlocke were appointed to the committee to present to King Charles I the propositions of the Treaty of Uxbridge, drawn up by Parliament in one of many attempts to end the Civil War. Their meeting with the King in Uxbridge, on the outskirts of London, sadly failed to end the war; the King was still too confident of success. The Treaty of Uxbridge named Sir Richard Grenville, amongst others, as one whose actions, even in the event of peace, would receive no pardon from Parliament.

In the midst of Cromwell's reign, in 1653, Maynard came to the defence of John Lilburne, known as 'Freeborn John', a political agitator who had been imprisoned repeatedly by Cromwell for his outspoken views on human rights. With Maynard's brilliant defence, Lilburn was acquitted, much to Cromwell's annoyance. Maynard had hoped to have Lilburne's support in his continuing case against Cromwell's brutal leadership, but Freeborn John declined the invitation.

Maynard's subsequent battles with Cromwell over *habeas corpus*-related issues put him in the Tower of London, but he seems to have re-gained favour with Cromwell, now reigning as Lord Protector of the Commonwealth, and John Maynard was appointed as the Protector's serjeant-at-law.

When Oliver Cromwell's son then inherited the Protectorship, Maynard found himself propping up a disastrous government, but his political mutability protected him. At the restoration of King Charles II, Maynard took part in the coronation procession as the new King's serjeant-at-law. Maynard was knighted, much to the derision of some of his anti-Royalist peers. Maynard was subsequently remembered for his greed, his fortune-hunting and his materialistic view of the world.[23] He became a very wealthy man.

In 1660 and 1661, Sir John Maynard was returned as MP for Bere Alston, just south of the Walreddon estates, along with George Howard, the son of Maynard's old friend George Cutteford.[24] South of Bere Alston is Bere Ferrers, where, in 1665, Sir John Maynard and his old enemy – and now business partner – Sir John Berkeley (then Lord Berkeley), amongst others, made a fortune in mining rights.[25] Sir John Maynard died in 1690, at the age of eighty-eight, at his vast estate of Gunnersbury Park, having survived three of his four wives and outliving all but one of his children.

———————————

In 1643, Sir William Russell, Mary Howard's cousin, also tried to negotiate peace with the King. Initially siding with Parliament, he defected to the King's forces in Oxford, and tried to persuade the King to open peace negotiations, but with limited success. The King was then in no mood for such negotiations.

Realising the situation was at that time hopeless, Russell returned to Parliament, but they were suspicious of his motives and refused to let him work with them again. Sir William returned to his family estate at Woburn Abbey, north-east of Oxford, and remained there for the rest of the war.

However, his younger brother, Edward Russell, remained in Oxford until June 1644. He was supposed to be command-

---

23 Alford, 1891.

24 George Howard was returned as a Member of Parliament for two constitu-encies in 1660: for Bere Alston, with Sir John Maynard, and for Tavistock, with Sir William Russell. George Howard chose to represent Tavistock, and another representative for Bere Alston was appointed to be the second repre-sentative with Sir John Maynard.

25 See the title deeds for their mining operations at Bere Ferrers, at Devon Record Office, ref 155M-0/T, dated 1665.

ing a regiment for Parliament[26], for his cousins the Howards, so the Parliamentary leaders were rightfully suspicious when they discovered Edward was living in William Day's house in St Aldgate in Oxford.[27] Edward Russell had been granted a licence to travel, to see relatives, but that licence had long expired. When asked by Parliament to explain himself, Edward could give no good reason for his presence in Oxford, secretly living with Royalists.

During 1644, besieged Oxford was filled with refugees and 'strangers'[28], who lived in any room they could find and who were conscripted to fight for the Royalists as they battled desperately against the attacking Parliamentary army. The King was rightly suspicious of some of these characters and requested that the Earl of Dorset do a survey of the local population, which produced some rather surprising results for both sides. There were a surprising number of Parliamentary supporters living in the Oxford tenements.

To Parliament, it seemed inexplicable that their officer, Edward Russell, would choose to stay in Oxford when he could be living more comfortably in London, or at his family estate of Woburn – or even taking part in the battles against the Royalists. They were, after all, employing him for that purpose. It seems very likely that Edward remained in Oxford as a spy for his older brother.

Sir William Howard, Mary Howard's brother-in-law, was also living in Oxford, just up the road from Edward Russell. Sir William had been commander of the King's personal guard at the Battle of Edgehill[29], while his nephews James, Earl of Suffolk, and his brother, George, were fighting for

---

26 Toynbee and Young, 1973, p. 61. Edward Russell was supposed to be commanding Carlisle's Regiment.

27 Toynbee and Young, 1973, p. 61.

28 Toynbee and Young, 1973. This is a remarkable study of the King's survey of the population of Oxford, concentrating on the few surviving documents which identify the residents of St Aldgate in Oxford. It brings to life the real problems of security in a city under siege.

29 Tinniswood, 2007, see footnote on p. 180.

Parliament.[30] Sir William lived in the same house as the King's apothecary – a rough tenement house in Oxford, just north of Christ Church, belonging to John Bolte, a tailor. It seemed a poor choice compared with the Howard family's vast estate at Audley End. But the King's survey of those residing in Oxford clearly states that, 'In parte of the house where John Bolte liveth Sir William Howard and 4 men'.[31] One of these anonymous and mysterious four men was possibly Sir William's nephew, the son of Mary Howard – George Halse.

George Halse was a man of many surnames, difficult to trace and difficult to pin down when it came to political allegiance. He was the ward of Francis Trelawney, the Trelawneys active in the support of King Charles I. He was also a Halse and a Howard, most of whom were fighting for Parliament. He was a man who disappeared during the war, probably acting as a spy and an informant, working with his friend William Russell in their efforts to end the war. But even he, regardless of the support of his relations Edward Russell and William Howard, could never have convinced King Charles I to request a hearing for a humble man like George Cutteford.

The essential piece on their chess board was George Cutteford's old friend, the Earl of Dorset, Lord Chamberlain to the King. Edward Sackville, a cousin to the Howards, had inherited the title of Earl of Dorset after the death of his brother Richard in 1614. Edward probably first met Mary when she married Charles Howard. They met again in 1628, at the Court of Queen Henrietta Maria, when Mary Howard was falling in love with Sir Richard Grenville. Edward Sackville was then Lord Chamberlain to the Queen, his wife governess to the royal children.

By 1628, Edward Sackville was already a firm friend of George Cutteford; they shared moderate views of religion

---

30 James, the Earl of Suffolk, and his brother Hon. George Howard fought for Parliament during the years 1642 until 1646, but were subsequently imprisoned as Royalists in 1647.

31 Toynbee and Young, 1973, p. 234.

and politics, and a fervent hatred of Richard Grenville. They also shared a common interest in acquiring land and money. Having inherited an impoverished estate from his brother, and desperate for good advice on contracts and accounts, George Cutteford was just the sort of friend Edward Sackville needed.

EDWARD SACKVILLE, EARL OF DORSET

Until he was thirty-four, in 1614, Edward Sackville had not expected to become the Earl of Dorset.[32] On the death of their father, the title had passed to Edward's older brother Richard, who was noted for his extravagance and profligacy. When Richard died, Edward inherited a title, a substantial, though impoverished, estate called Knole in Kent and a series of debts. Fortunately for the family estate, Edward was 'a sober and consistent gentleman'[33] and a fiercely loyal servant to King Charles I, travelling in Europe and the New World to secure the fortunes of his sovereign, and a little money for himself. He was a cousin to Theophilus Howard, and both were active members of the King's Privy Council. At the start of the English Civil War, Edward Sackville was employed as Lord Chamberlain to the Queen, with his wife governess to the royal children. This essentially put them in charge of the royal household. Edward took part in the Battle of Edgehill in 1642, fighting courageously for the Royalists. He was the bodyguard for the royal children amidst the terrifying slaughter. Meanwhile his family estate at Knole in Kent was ransacked, desecrated and sequestered by Parliament's forces.

By 1644, Sackville was Lord Chamberlain to the King, representing the King in the newly-constituted Oxford Parliament while the King was travelling with his army,

---

32 Sackville-West, 1922, and Sackville-West, 2010. Both give excellent accounts of the life of Edward Sackville, though quite different in style.

33 Sackville-West, 1922, p. 96.

and also leading the negotiations for peace with Parliament. He had the King's ear throughout the war, whether or not the King was willing to listen to Edward's constant and persuasive pleas for an end to the conflict.

His position, though, put his sons in great danger. His elder son, Richard was captured and imprisoned by Parliament in the early stages of the war, and his younger son, Edward, an active soldier during the battles, was kidnapped at Kidlington near Oxford and brutally murdered there by Parliamentary soldiers.

Despite his criticism of the war, and his own personal tragedies, Edward Sackville remained loyal to the King throughout the war. When King Charles I was beheaded in 1649, Edward returned to Knole, vowing never to set foot outside his estate again – he kept his vow, and died in 1652.

When Sir Richard Grenville attacked Edward Courtenay in 1630, it was the Earl of Dorset on the Privy Council who issued the warrant, and, with his cousin the Earl of Suffolk, he actively supported Mary Howard and George Cutteford in their battles against Sir Richard.

When the Civil War broke out, Edward Sackville argued against the conflict, and took an active part in peace negotiations throughout the war. He remained loyal to the King, travelling with the King's army to the battle of Edgehill, and then to Oxford to establish the King's new Parliament there. In 1644, he was Lord Chamberlain, an important adviser, though the King was not always one to listen to counsel.

When George Cutteford was imprisoned at Lydford and then in Exeter, Cutteford's petitions for release could have reached the Earl of Dorset from many sources – William Russell's younger brother Edward, or Sir William Howard (both staying in Oxford in 1644). George Halse/Howard would certainly have ensured the petitions for his father's release reached Dorset.

However, even with these pieces in place, an obstacle remained. The conflict made it difficult for men to travel – they had to obtain a licence from the Parliament, or the King where appropriate, giving them permission to be on the road, or to enter any city. Oxford was constantly under siege, so getting through Parliament's forces surrounding Oxford, then being given permission to enter Oxford itself was no easy matter. Transporting George Cutteford's petitions to the Earl of Dorset, to be brought to the King's attention, was fraught with many dangers.

The only person, of all George Cutteford's many connections, could have achieved this feat – Lady Mary Howard.

THE SOCIETY OF LADY MARY HOWARD, 1644

In Oxford
The Earl of Dorset, Edward Sackville, Lord Chamberlain to King Charles I
Sir William Howard, her brother-in-law, commander of the King's personal guard and uncle to James Howard, 4th Earl of Suffolk (working for Parliament)
Sir William Russell, also her brother-in-law, who was negotiating peace with the King. He was a Royalist in 1643, but returned to Parliament in 1644, residing at Woburn Abbey, north of Oxford
Edward Russell, her brother-in-law, the younger brother of Sir William Russell (working for Parliament)
Sir William Courtenay, her sixteen-year-old nephew, just released from Rougemont Castle in Exeter (and fighting for the King)

In London
Sir John Maynard, friend of George Cutteford, who was negotiating peace with King Charles I on behalf of Parliament

George Halse/ Howard, her son by George Cutteford.
George possibly moved to Oxford with Sir William Russell

In Plymouth
Grace Cutteford, wife to George Cutteford
George Cutteford the younger, son of George Cutteford
(fighting for Parliament)
John Cutteford, son of George Cutteford

In Exeter
Sir John Berkeley, Governor of Exeter, an old friend and
ally of the Earl of Dorset
George Cutteford, the elder, prisoner transferred from
Lydford Gaol sometime in July 1644

———————————

Women were permitted to travel without the appropriate
licences. As they were considered to have no active involvement in the war, they could move across the country more
easily than men. It was not unusual for women to join their
husbands near the battlefields or travel to visit relatives. It was
dangerous – the roads were still not safe for unwary travellers – but their journeys were rarely questioned by the soldiers
patrolling the highways. In the seventeenth century, it was generally accepted that a loyal wife should be with her husband,
and many officers' wives made terrifying journeys through
cities under siege to be with their husbands and families.

Despite her straitened circumstances, Lady Mary Howard
must have travelled to Plymouth, by ship, into a harbour
constantly under cannon-fire from besieging Royalists, to
discover where George Cutteford was being held. If she travelled directly to Exeter, her marriage to Sir Richard Grenville
would ironically have given her easy access.

Very likely it was Mary Howard who arranged Cutteford's
transfer from Lydford Gaol to Rougemont Castle in Exeter,
probably with assistance from the Earl of Dorset. Sir John

Berkeley was Governor at Exeter at the time, having besieged the Parliamentary forces there and taken the city in September 1643. Sir John Berkeley was not only a good friend of the Earl of Dorset, but he owed the Earl of Dorset a favour.

In 1641, Sir John had found himself imprisoned by Parliament for conspiracy in the Army Plots, an alleged plot by the King's officers to bring the northern army into London and so take Parliament by force. Sir John Berkeley was in a tight spot; his life at stake, and it was the Earl of Dorset who bailed him out, paying Parliament the enormous sum of £10,000 to free him. Sir John Berkeley owed Edward Sackville a very big favour. Having George Cutteford transferred to Exeter sometime in June 1644, and subsequently supporting Cutteford's case – and Berkeley's prominent support for Cutteford's case was exceptional – was probably that favour.

Mary Howard must have then travelled back to London and made her way through the fighting up to Oxford to deliver the petition from George Cutteford, with the added backing of Sir John Berkeley. Though her situation was precarious, certainly dangerous, she merely had to convince the guards at Oxford that she was visiting her relatives there, and they would have let her through. Her influential contacts gave her access to many of the cities under siege.

In her efforts, Mary would have recruited the support of many of her friends and relatives, including the Courtenays, the Earl of Dorset, Sir John Maynard, Sir William Russell and his brother, and the Howards – including her own son, George Halse – all of whom not only wanted to see George Cutteford released, but also wanted to see Sir Richard Grenville's shining success as a war hero turned to dust.

All of this is, of course, speculation, based on circumstantial evidence, perhaps inspired only by coincidental dates and locations, because the very key to Mary's success was that her travels remained unrecorded and unnoticed by both sides in the conflict.

George Cutteford's first petition sadly had little effect, but by the end of September 1644, the King's impression of Sir Richard

Grenville had markedly changed. The King, like many Royalists, suspected that Sir Richard was embezzling from the war funds to create a professional army, who answered only to Grenville. There had never been a professional army before in England, and those in charge on both sides of the conflict did not want one now. A professional army, they felt, would take power from the King and from Parliament. A professional army could mean, in the midst of the chaos, a military takeover of the country. A professional army was something to be afraid of, and that was exactly what Sir Richard Grenville was establishing in the south west. His men were paid by him and therefore loyal only to him. They were no longer fighting for King and country; they were fighting for their employer. Two professional armies were growing on opposite sides of the war, and the moderates were between them, desperately negotiating peace settlements, anxious to prevent any kind of military coup.

They failed.

However, they did manage to discredit Richard Grenville, who never again held a senior position in the King's forces. In 1647, the New Model Army seized London, despite the opposition of the Presbyterians – Sir John Maynard amongst them – and effectively took control of the country.

OLIVER CROMWELL

Born in Huntingdon in 1599 into the middle classes, an inheritance from his uncle brought Oliver Cromwell an education at Cambridge University and he soon converted to Puritanism. As MP for Cambridge in 1640, he sought reforms in the Church and Parliament, and as Civil War broke out, he became one of the most vocal leaders in Parliaments' fight against the King, and a key military leader, bringing Parliament many successes on the battlefield.

Cromwell established the New Model Army, bringing about the defeat of the Royalists, and the dissolution of the

Monarchy and the Church of England. He signed the death warrant of King Charles I and then tried in vain to establish a new form of government, with strict religious leaders. His idealistic aim was to govern the country with improved laws, supported by a moral foundation in Puritan values. He believed it was God's will he should lead the country, but his religious intolerance, imprisonments without trial and his vicious attacks on Ireland were no different then his predecessor. The country lived in fear. His 'Commonwealth' failed, with factions arguing and falling into chaos, and in frustration he took control of the country as Lord Protector.

His reign lasted until his own death in 1658, when his son inherited the role, to great public and political distrust. Sir John Maynard continued to support the new government as best he could, as it fell into disarray, but happily changed his allegiance to the restoration of the monarchy and the coronation of King Charles II in 1660.

————————

What did the moderates do then? Sir John Maynard worked for the new Parliament under Cromwell, still trying to undermine Cromwell's authority, but failing. Sir William Russell returned to his Woburn estates for the rest of the war, remaining there until the restoration of the King in 1660, when he took up his role as MP for Tavistock. Edward Sackville, Earl of Dorset, after the execution of the King, remained at his Knole estates and died in 1652. They had failed and there was nothing more they could do.

Mary Howard, having delivered her successful petition, returned to Fitzford – and redecorated. She probably felt she and her son had 'done their bit'; now they wanted simply to return to peace and quiet in Devon. Mary managed the Fitz estates and made a home for her son. For the rest of her life, she did nothing but live the life of a grand lady.

And then, in 1671, at the age of forty-nine, George Howard died. His own son had died in infancy, so his Howard line died with him. Hearing the news of her son's death, Mary Howard, now seventy-five, became distraught and took to her bed. She had nothing left to live for. As Mary Howard lay there, she was visited by her cousin, Sir William Courtenay. Sir William had married young and now had nineteen children to look after. His estates at Powderham were in disarray, with little money left for the necessary re-building work, but here was his chance to restore the Courtenay fortunes.

They discussed her will. Now her son was dead, there was no one left to inherit all her property: 4,000 acres in four counties, and a further personal fortune of nearly £10,000. She signed a new will, signed her name 'Mary Grenville' and bequeathed to William Courtenay all of her estates.[34] After 134 years, Okehampton Park was at last back in the hands of the Courtenay family.

Mary Howard turned her face to the wall and died.

---

34 D1508M-11/F/1 and D1508M-11/F/2, both dated 1671, both held at Devon Record Office.

Chapter Eleven

A Spirited Lady

In 1677, John Cutteford, younger son of George Cutteford the elder, wrote to Richard Sackville. Richard was the 5th Earl of Dorset, after the death of his father Edward and John Cutteford was looking for work. John was growing old, and the life of a customs officer was too much for him now. It is likely he asked for assistance from Richard Sackville in memory of the friendship between their two fathers.

Richard Sackville graciously found the old man employment as Warden of Sackville College in Sussex, an almshouse established by his grandfather, now one of the finest Jacobean homes still existing in England. The College had suffered some problems with financial irregularities and, remembering how

Church of Ottery St Mary.

George Cutteford had befriended Edward Sackville so many years before, Richard would have seen John Cutteford as the ideal man for the job. Who better than the son of George Cutteford to sort out the mess? He felt that John Cutteford could be trusted, and indeed John did a good job in the last three years of his life.

Many years after John Cutteford died, the new Warden of Sackville College discovered an old chest, and put a notice in the paper asking if anyone knew anything about it. It contained letters from a Mary Howard to someone called George Cutteford, and many other papers pertaining to the Cutteford family. It seems that John Cutteford had kept everything: every letter and document that would remind him of the life he never had. It was from the papers from this chest that, in 1890, Mrs Radford would write her history of Lady Howard for the Devonshire Association[1], ironically not realising that it was quite possible she herself was married to a descendant of that same George Cutteford.[2]

The accounts John Cutteford left behind reveal that his life had been plagued by financial difficulties and disappointments.[3] He had been arrested by the Sheriff of Devon for non-payment of debt. He had inherited legacies from his sisters as they passed away, but he was constantly weighed down by money worries. He had once owned land, but the tenants had been unable to pay him and he had had to have them arrested. He had argued with a Halse cousin, and had had to pay him off. He had been charged with contempt by the Court of Chancery and duly fined. He had received no help from the Howards, yet he had kept all his father's papers, and the letters Mary Howard had lovingly sent George Cutteford.

1   Radford, 1890.

2   I have not endeavoured to research the Radford family tree, but it is interesting to note that George Cutteford's daughter had two sons George and Robert Radford, and there are still Radfords, it seems, living in Whitchurch today.

3   Add Ms 18008-826, undated though circa 1660, held at West Sussex Record Office.

He himself left no children, no wife, just a chest of ageing and decaying documents that implied his resentment at the downward spiral of his fortunes; the bitterness he felt at the thought of the life he might have had, if his father had lived.

John Cutteford's life was one of disappointment. In the early years, John's father, born of lowly status, was presented with opportunities and possibilities unheard of in previous generations. Suddenly the elder George Cutteford was a man of rising status. From a charitable school, George Cutteford became an important man, with prestigious connections, and through his own hard work, his own endeavours, albeit with a hint of self-interest and a touch of corruption typical of the times, he had risen to become one of the new affluent middle classes.

The early seventeenth century promised great prosperity for everyone. The Puritan faith promised a bold new future, with developments in education, freedom of thought and religion. For the first time in British history, the working classes felt they could realise their potential and improve the prospects for their children. The bonds of social and economic status that had held them down for so long were just beginning to break – not completely, but there was a hint of something better.

Universal suffrage, even for all men, let alone women, was unheard of, but the idea was planted, that perhaps one day they would all have a say in how the country was governed, affecting and amending those laws and regulations that so often blighted their lives.

Changes that would not occur until the nineteenth century were being passionately discussed in the seventeenth. The opening of the New World, new horizons, brought unheard of prosperity and aspirations to many. Here was a world of new possibilities, where people like the Cuttefords could aspire to own their land and be connected with people outside their limited social sphere.

The Civil War arose from these aspirations, from the rise of the learned advisers contesting the absolute power of the King.

Arguments over money, power and religion fractured the country, but still the people believed they could affect a change. Drawn into horrific battles, they often sacrificed their own lives, and the lives of their sons, to make that change happen. They fought over ideas and the processes for change.

Sadly, some of those in charge, like Sir Richard Grenville, felt that the war and the subsequent breakdown in society was an opportunity to make money, and left them unaccountable, exacting personal justice against those who could not defend themselves. Sir Richard destroyed those same protagonists for change – including George Cutteford and his family, who represented everything men like Grenville hated in the burgeoning new society.

Parliament won the war in the end, and many thought that the anticipated changes would arise from that new government. Others, like Sir John Maynard, realised all too quickly that nothing was going to change after all, and those who had sought change had won nothing, their victory stolen from them by the old establishment and a military dictatorship in the form of Oliver Cromwell. The men who took the powers from a King were themselves despotic, intolerant and as unwilling to seek social changes as the King had been.

In 1650, it must have felt like progress had been completely reversed. Suddenly it was more like the fifteenth century than the seventeenth. Land may have changed hands, but it was still only landowners who were permitted to sit in Parliament and govern the country. There was not even a gesture towards universal representation. Those without land were still no better off than they had been 200 years before.

After years of death and destruction, of sacrifice and starvation, it was back to 'business as usual', though a business now more rigid in its laws, and the population dominated by Cromwell's intolerance. And worse was to come. Soon anyone not agreeing with Cromwell was ousted from Parliament, and he ruled the 1650s as Lord Protector, a substitute King, even nominating his son as his hereditary successor.

And John Cutteford was back where it all started, in his father's old trade, as a customs officer. When King Charles II was crowned in 1660, to John Cutteford and his relations still in Tavistock, it must have been as though the Civil War had never happened. The Radfords and the Halses and the Skirretts kept going, but there was little sign of progress. The contracts, the land deals, the hard work, the New World, the battles, the thousands dead – all of it had achieved absolutely nothing. The struggle for social and economic change had to begin all over again.

So who did the people like John Cutteford blame for all this? London was a distant place, too far away in society as well as in miles. Kings and Lord Protectors were all beyond their sphere of influence; out of sight, out of mind. So they turned their sights on the ostentatiously wealthy local land-owner – Mary Howard – and saw a woman who had returned to Fitzford, and had done nothing since for anyone but herself.

Mary Howard spent the years after the war redecorating; she restored, she collected the rent, often from those who could not afford it, and she travelled around the town in a sedan chair, oblivious, it seems, to the suffering of the local people around her. She sat in church in all her finery, watching silently as the Puritan priests were expelled after the restoration of the King; witnessing a generation of people having to start over again with less wealth than their forefathers.

After the death of Richard Grenville, their daughter Elizabeth fell onto hard times. Her husband, Captain Lennard, a Royalist, died, and Elizabeth petitioned King Charles II for support for her child, but received only a single payment of £100. Her baby subsequently died, and Elizabeth, it is said, then visited Fitzford to ask for her mother's help.

Mary refused to acknowledge the woman as her daughter. Elizabeth had lived for so many years with her father, in Europe, tending him in his old age, that Mary no longer recognised the woman claiming to be her daughter. Elizabeth pleaded with Mary, tugging on her mother's skirts as Mary climbed the stairs at Fitzford. At the top of the stairs, Mary turned and violently slammed the door in Elizabeth's face. Mary did eventually bequeath some money in her will to Elizabeth – but only if the woman could prove she was indeed her daughter. Mary Howard's final years were filled with contempt and indifference.

THE FINAL VICTORY OF SIR RICHARD GRENVILLE

Sir Richard, in Exeter in 1645, having seen the death of his old enemy George Cutteford, recovered from his wounds, but the King and his Council were still unhappy with Richard's conduct in Devon, and Richard's behaviour for the remainder of the war did his career no favours. His troops at Taunton deserted in huge numbers – only 600 of the original 2,000 remained. They hadn't been paid while Sir Richard was convalescing, so many simply went back home to Cornwall.

While the King's forces were being sorely defeated by Cromwell's New Model Army at Naseby, in June 1644, and the Royalists subsequently besieged at Taunton, Richard was of no help. He spent most of his time bickering with Sir John Berkeley in Exeter, and General Goring, leader of the King's forces.

In a huff, Sir Richard resigned his commission and took himself off to Ottery St Mary, near Exeter, with about 350 men in tow, and set about raising funds there, using the same violent and abusive methods for raising money from the local population as he had done so often before. He did manage to recruit additional forces in defence of Devon and Cornwall, and in October 1645, with 2,500 men at his command, Sir Richard fortified Okehampton in opposition to an imminent attack by Parliamentary forces heading into the west. The defences failed.

Prince Charles called Sir Richard to meet with him at Launceston, but the bickering continued, and

Prince Charles, exasperated by the persistently uncoopera-
tive Grenville, had Sir Richard imprisoned at Launceston
Gaol for insubordination, and then transferred to St
Michael's Mount in Cornwall. As Parliament's forces ominously advanced into Cornwall, Sir Richard managed to
escape to France, leaving behind his possessions; they were
subsequently ransacked by the Parliamentary soldiers.

In the following year, Sir Richard and his son, also
named Richard Grenville, made a desperate journey back
to England in an attempt it seems to raise money from the
Fitz estates.[4] Sir Richard travelled in disguise, wearing a
long periwig and dying his beard black, in an effort not to
be captured by Cromwell's men. The journey would end
in tragedy, however, as the younger Richard Grenville was
caught robbing passengers on the highway and Parliament
had him executed as a highwayman at Tyburn.[5]

Sir Richard Grenville died in 1659, exiled in the
Netherlands, cared for by his daughter Elizabeth.
Impoverished and in ill health in the last years of his life,
he still managed to exact some small revenge against his
old enemy, the Earl of Suffolk. During the English Civil
War, the Earl of Suffolk had sent some expensive tapestries
and Turkish carpets, worth £27,000, as payment of a debt
to a merchant in Holland. While the carpets were stored
in Bruges, Sir Richard had them seized – as repayment, he
declared, for monies the Earl of Suffolk's family still owed
him from 1640. Sir Richard travelled to Bruges, broke down
the warehouse doors and took the lot.

Sir Richard was of course accused of theft, and the case
dragged on for many years. At the time of his death, Sir
Richard was still in possession of £27,000 worth of carpets that had once belonged to the Earl of Suffolk. It was

---

4   Radford, 1890, p 101, and Miller, 1979, p145 and 146. Miller gives quite a
    detailed account of Sir Richard's journey to and through England, though
    no-one seems to be able to identify his reasons for the visit.

5   Miller, 1979, p. 145.

a small, petty victory, typical of a man who had stolen so much from so many.[6]

All around Fitzford were impoverished tenements and still Mary Howard did nothing. When she died, the ghostly stories of Lady Howard of Tavistock began.

Mary Howard became the urban legend of the white lady, haunting the Dartmoor roads. It is said she also haunts the grounds at Walreddon, but her ride from Tavistock to Okehampton is how she is remembered. But it is a strange haunting, so unlike other stories of ghostly 'white ladies' who frequent those places where they have lost lovers or died waiting for their lovers to return. They are often seen in mourning, saddened by actions that should or should not have been taken. They are poignant stories of love and loss.

There is, they say, a 'white lady' in the ruins of Radford Park, once home to Mary Howard's grandmother. This 'white lady' drowned in the lake there, having met on a boat with a female friend of a lower class, despite her family's disapproval. And now she haunts the shores of Radford Lake, seeking out her friend, an expression of yearning and tragic death at such a young age. The traditional 'white lady' is an image of how love survives despite the tragedy of separation and death.

Lady Howard's ride is of a different composition. She does not choose to haunt, nor appears to mourn her loss. She is no self-determined spirit refusing to leave until she has found her lover/ friend/ family. She is not depicted as a mournful lady making epic journeys to save the life of her lover. Instead, she is condemned to ride on a pointless journey night after night, on a

---

6   Miller, 1979, p. 159. Elizabeth, Sir Richard's daughter, was caring for her father at the time of his death. After his death, she had the carpets and tapestries returned to their rightful owner. Sir Richard died on 22 October 1659, just as his nephew, Sir John Grenville, was negotiating for the return of the monarchy.

never-ending mission, plucking grass from Okehampton Park. Her journey is an exercise in futility. The story could also be seen as symbolic of the seventeenth century itself – an arduous journey of pointless endeavour that takes the traveller back to where she started.

The story has of course been embellished over the years, now with a black devil dog and a headless driver, and hideous skulls decorating the coach. The most recent addition is peculiar to the twenty-first century. One witness said they saw a spectral figure in the coach with Mary: a pale, faceless phantom combing Mary's hair. Perhaps this is her daughter, Elizabeth, finally reconciled. Perhaps this is just the wishful thinking of a new generation, hoping no one will have to make such a terrible journey alone.

Mary Howard, in fact, never rode from Tavistock to Okehampton in a coach – the Devon roads of the seventeenth century were too treacherous for coaches, and she never even owned such a vehicle. But still the legend persists.

In time, a rhyme was written, and recorded in the works of Sabine Baring-Gould, with verses added over the centuries. It is a rhyme full of bitterness. It has the tone of a jilted lover condemning the cause of his ruination to perpetual suffering. The pain is in the repetition, the cycle repeated over and over.

> My ladye hath a sable coach,
> And horses two and four;
> My ladye hath a black blood-hound
> That runneth on before.

> My ladye's coach hath nodding plumes,
> The driver hath no head;
> My ladye is an ashen white,
> As one that long is dead.

'Now pray step in!' my ladye saith,
'Now pray step in and ride.'
I thank thee, I had rather walk
Than gather to thy side.

The wheels go round without a sound,
Or tramp of turn of wheels;
As cloud at night, in pale moonlight,
Along the carriage steals.

'Now pray step in!' my ladye saith,
'Now prithee come to me.'
She takes the baby from the crib,
She sits it on her knee.

'Now pray step in!' my ladye saith,
'Now pray step in and ride.'
Then deadly pale, in waving veil,
She takes to her the bride.

'Now pray step in!' my ladye saith,
'There's room I wot for you.'
She wav'd her hand, the coach did stand,
The Squire within she drew.

'Now pray step in!' my ladye saith,
'Why shouldst thou trudge afoot?'
She took the gaffer in by her,
His crutches in the boot.

I'd rather walk a hundred miles,
And run by night and day,
Than have that carriage halt for me
And hear my ladye say –

'Now pray step in, and make no din,
Step in with me to ride;
There's room, I trow, by me for you,
And all the world beside.'[7]

A gatehouse still stands where Mary Howard once lived.
The big house is gone. Now it's all cottages with chickens
and such, and schoolrooms on the other side of the brook.
If you go by the Plymouth road to Tavistock, you'll see it, that
gatehouse, hidden in plain sight. Wait there until midnight,
and the lady herself will appear, pale as sour milk in her fine
silk. Four times the bride, dead heart inside. Then comes her
coach, which Satan himself has made for her – according to
the legend – from the skin and bones of her last husband's
victims, crowned with their fiery skulls to light her way. Along
the dark and winding road she rides, screaming past the old
gaol at Lydford, then out across the moors to the blood-soaked
walls of Okehampton Castle. Again and again, she makes that
journey. Night after long night, while the ghosts of hanging
men wait for her at Lydford gaol. Perhaps George Cutteford is
still trapped there with them, still seeking justice, and waiting
in the cold and dark for Mary Howard to come and find him
and take him home.

If you see the white lady, beware she does not see you lin-
gering on the road. For she will stop, the coach door fly open,
and her withered hand reach out and beckon you to join her.
'There's room, I trow, by me for you, And all the world beside.'

---

7 This version reproduced from Baring-Gould, 1908. There are many other
  excellent versions, including a traditional song.

Timeline

1538   Okehampton Castle destroyed by King Henry VIII, and Henry Courtenay beheaded for treason

1558   Queen Elizabeth I ascends to the throne

1576   Sir John Fitz, father to Mary, born

1582   William Cutteford writes his will

1588   King Philip II of Spain sends the Spanish Armada to invade England, only to be defeated by the English Navy under Sir Francis Drake

1590   Sir John Fitz's father dies, and Sir Arthur Gorges becomes his guardian.

1595   John Fitz marries Bridget Courtenay and they move to Fitzford. Meanwhile, Richard Halse, agent to Bridget's grandfather, Sir William Courtenay, moves into nearby Walreddon with his family

1596   Birth of Mary Fitz at Walreddon

1591   Sir Richard Grenville, the privateer, grandfather of Sir Richard Grenville of the English Civil War, dies heroically on his ship *Revenge*, under fire from the Spanish fleet.

1599   George Cutteford, customs officer, marries Grace Halse, daughter of Nicholas Halse and they settle in Plympton

       John Fitz murders Nicholas Slanning

1600   Birth of Sir Richard Grenville

1601-1603 English Lords violently suppress the uprisings at the Munster Plantations in Ireland

1603   Queen Elizabeth I dies; James VI of Scotland becomes King James I of England and Scotland

Sir William Courtenay the younger dies on his return
from the uprisings in Ireland

1605 John Fitz murders Daniel Alley and commits suicide
Mary Fitz becomes a ward of the 9th Earl of
Northumberland, and is taken to Syon House
Gunpowder Plot discovered, 9th Earl of
Northumberland imprisoned
Mary Fitz taken to London to live with Lady Hatton

1606 Sir Alan Percy purchases Mary Fitz's wardship

1608 Mary Fitz married off to Sir Alan Percy

1607 George Cutteford established as an attorney in Tavistock

1611 Sir Alan Percy dies, Bridget Courtenay dies

1612 Mary Fitz marries Thomas Darcy; Thomas Darcy dies
October: Mary Fitz marries Sir Charles Howard

1613 Mary has her first child, Elizabeth, who dies young

1614 Mary has her second child, Mary, who eventually marries into the Vernon family and settles in London
The 'Addled Parliament' of King James I

1616 Death of William Shakespeare

1617 Frances Coke, daughter of Lady Hatton, forced to
marry Sir John Villiers, insane younger brother of the
Duke of Buckingham

1619 Sir Thomas Howard, 1st Earl of Suffolk and Lord High
Treasurer, arrested and imprisoned for embezzlement

1620 Charles Howard and his wife Mary separate
The Pilgrim Fathers sail from Plymouth on the
Mayflower to the New World

1622 Mary has her third child, George Halse, son of George
Cutteford

1623 The Halses vacate Walreddon, taking George Halse
with them

1625 King James I dies; King Charles I ascends to the throne
King Charles I marries the Catholic Henrietta Maria,
daughter of Henry IV of France

1626 Sir Thomas Howard, 1st Earl of Suffolk dies in London,
the title passing to his eldest son Theophilus Howard

Sir Charles Howard dies in Tavistock
Plague kills hundreds in Tavistock
Sir Francis Courtenay appointed Lord Warden of the
Stannaries

1627 Mary Howard takes her brother-in-law, Theophilus
Howard, to court

1628 King Charles I reluctantly signs Parliament's Petition of
Right, designed to protect subjects from any taxation
not authorised by Parliament
George Villers, Duke of Buckingham, assassinated by
naval lieutenant John Felton
Sir Richard Grenville marries Mary Howard (née Fitz)
George Cutteford the younger purchases Tiddy Brook
Farm in Whitchurch, and enters the Middle Temple in
London
George Cutteford the elder and his family take up resi-
dence at Walreddon.

1629 While debating the Petition of Right, King Charles I
dismisses Parliament, and then arrests nine members of
the House of Commons for offences against the state,
declaring that *habeas corpus* does not apply to the King

1630 Mary gives birth to a son, called Richard Grenville
after his father
Richard Grenville arrested and imprisoned for assault
against Edward Courtenay
Sir William Courtenay, trustee of the Fitz estates, dies
in London, during the investigation
The Earl of Pembroke, co-trustee to the Fitz estates, dies
George Halse is discovered by the Court of Wards,
declared to be the son and heir of Sir Charles Howard,
and made a ward of Sir Francis Trelawney at Lamerton

1631 Richard Grenville released from prison
Mary gives birth to a daughter, Elizabeth Grenville,
and leaves for London to escape her abusive husband
Mary Howard and Sir Richard Grenville formally
separate

1632   Sir Richard Grenville and George Cutteford imprisoned
       in the Fleet prison in London, on separate charges

1633   King Charles I appoints Archbishop Laud, a Catholic
       sympathiser, to quell the rise of Puritanism

1638   Sir Francis Courtenay dies. Sir William Courtenay, his
       son, becomes a ward of his mother, who marries Amos
       Ameredith
       Parliament challenges King Charles I's right to levy
       Ship Money on inland towns
       King Charles I demands that the Book of Common
       Prayer be used in the Scottish Kirk. Subsequent riots
       and the formation of the National Covenant, expelling
       the bishops from Scotland. Scottish forces invade the
       north of England

1639   Sir Richard Grenville returns to London, and sues
       Theophilus Howard

1640   Charles recalls Parliament to raise funds for a war on
       Scotland
       The Earl of Strafford leads an army against Scotland, but
       the army mutinies, leaving English land in Scottish hands
       Theophilus Howard, Earl of Suffolk, dies
       Sir Richard Grenville reclaims Fitzford

1641   Parliament has Strafford executed for treason
       Revolt and uprisings in Ireland. Protestant English set-
       tlers driven from their homes, and Parliament sends an
       army to quell the uprising
       Sir Richard Grenville sent to fight in Ireland
       John Pym prepares the Grand Remonstrance, a list of
       Parliament's grievances against the King since his reign
       began

1642   King Charles I has five members of the House of
       Commons, including John Pym, arrested.
       Parliament take control of the militia. Charles attempts
       to secure an arsenal in Hull, but is forced to retire to
       York, establishing his headquarters there as the country
       heads for Civil War

August: War is declared. Royalists versus Parliament
Plymouth declares for Parliament and prepares fortifications to defend itself against a lengthy Royalist
siege
October: Battle of Edgehill results in stalemate
King Charles establishes his new capital at Oxford,
which is besieged by Parliament

1643   Sir Richard Grenville returns from Ireland and declares
his support for Parliament
Royalists have victories at Braddock Down and Nantwich
Parliament take Lichfield, Reading, Wakefield and
Gainsborough
Royalist take Ripple Field, Tewkesbury, Chewton
Mendip, Chalgrove Field, Lansdowne Hill, Bristol and
Yorkshire, retake Lichfield and Gainsborough and hold
Newark, Devises and Cornwall
Royalists take Exeter after a long siege
First battle of Newbury, Parliamentarian victory

1644   Earl of Dorset appointed King's Lord Chamberlain
March: Sir Richard Grenville dramatically changes side,
returning to the King's forces. The King sends him into
Devon to recruit for the Royalist army
March: Sir Richard expels George Cutteford and
his family from Walreddon and imprisons George
Cutteford at Lydford Gaol
April: Sir Richard Grenville arrests Sir William
Courtenay and sends him to be imprisoned at
Rougemont Castle
June: Queen Henrietta Maria gives birth to a daughter
at Exeter, and flees to France
July: George Cutteford transferred to Rougemont
Castle in Exeter. Writes his will
September: Battle of Lostwithiel, a Royalist Victory
September: Joseph Grenville, son of Sir Richard
Grenville, hanged in Plymouth as a traitor
November: George Cutteford hearing before the

King's commissioners, in the Chapter House at Exeter
November: Attempt at peace settlement, with the
Treaty of Uxbridge, brought by Sir John Maynard to
the King Charles I

1645 Sir Richard Grenville's final major attack on Plymouth
fails
Siege of Taunton; Sir Richard Grenville wounded and
returns to Exeter.
April: George Cutteford dies
June: Battle of Naseby, Parliament victory
July: Sir William Courtenay wounded at the Battle of
Bridgewater

1646 April: Exeter falls to Parliament
April: George Cutteford, the younger, dies
King Charles I surrenders to the Scots, who subse-
quently hand him over to Parliament and imprisonment
Oxford surrenders to Parliament

1649 Rump Parliament established, and all those in favour of
negotiating with the King expelled

1649 30 January: King Charles I executed at Whitehall
Palace, London. Formation of the Commonwealth

1652 Earl of Dorset dies

1653 Oliver Cromwell appointed Lord Protector of the
Commonwealth

1655 George Howard marries Mary Burnby, who dies in
childbirth. The baby dies months later

1656 Court of Wards abolished

1658 Oliver Cromwell dies

1660 Restoration of the Monarchy. King Charles II crowned
in London
George Howard nominated as an MP for Tavistock
with Sir William Russell, his uncle, and at the same
time nominated to represent Bere Alston with his old
friend Sir John Maynard. George Howard chooses to
represent Tavistock

1665 Grace Cutteford finally signs the lease for the

Walreddon estate over to George Howard for the sum of £300

1671 George Howard dies

Mary Howard dies. The Fitz estates are bequeathed to Sir William Courtenay

1677 John Cutteford appointed as Warden of Sackville College

1680 John Cutteford dies

1690 Sir John Maynard, attorney to King Charles I, serjeant-at-law to Oliver Cromwell and to King Charles II, dies

Family Trees

The Courtenays of Powderham*

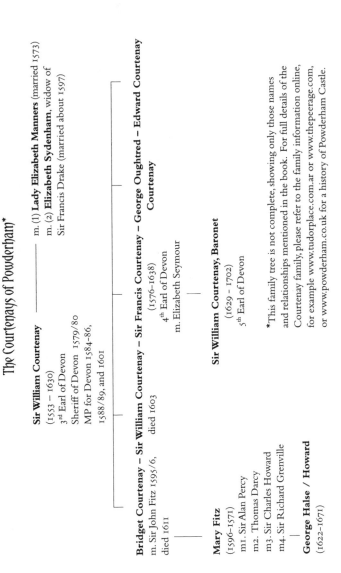

Sir William Courtenay
(1553 – 1630)
3rd Earl of Devon
Sheriff of Devon 1579/80
MP for Devon 1584–86,
1588/89, and 1601

m. (1) **Lady Elizabeth Manners** (married 1573)
m. (2) **Elizabeth Sydenham**, widow of
Sir Francis Drake (married about 1597)

Bridget Courtenay – Sir William Courtenay – Sir Francis Courtenay – George Oughtred – Edward Courtenay
m. Sir John Fitz 1595/6,   died 1603   (1576–1638)   Courtenay
died 1611   4th Earl of Devon
                                                                 m. Elizabeth Seymour

Mary Fitz
(1596–1571)
m1. Sir Alan Percy
m2. Thomas Darcy
m3. Sir Charles Howard
m4. Sir Richard Grenville

George Halse / Howard
(1622–1671)

Sir William Courtenay, Baronet
(1629 – 1702)
5th Earl of Devon

*This family tree is not complete, showing only those names
and relationships mentioned in the book. For full details of the
Courtenay family, please refer to the family information online,
for example www.tudorplace.com.ar or www.thepeerage.com,
or www.powderham.co.uk for a history of Powderham Castle.

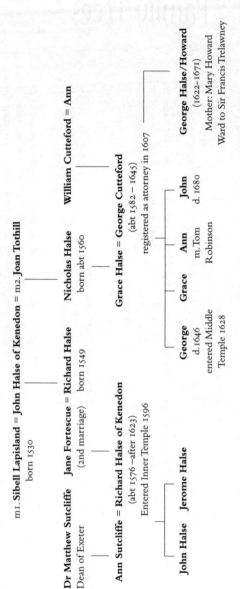

The Cutteford and Halse families*

m1. **Sibell Lapisland** = **John Halse of Kenedon** = m2. **Joan Tothill**
born 1530

Dr Matthew Sutcliffe   **Jane Fortescue** = **Richard Halse**   **Nicholas Halse**   **William Cutteford** = **Ann**
Dean of Exeter   (2nd marriage)   born 1549   born abt 1560

Ann Sutcliffe = **Richard Halse of Kenedon**   **Grace Halse** = **George Cutteford**
                 (abt 1576 –after 1623)   (abt 1582 – 1645)
                 Entered Inner Temple 1596   registered as attorney in 1607

John Halse   Jerome Halse

George   **Grace**   **Ann**   **John**   **George Halse/Howard**
d.1646   m.Tom   d. 1680   (1622–1671)
entered Middle   Robinson   Mother: Mary Howard
Temple 1628   Ward to Sir Francis Trelawney

*This family tree is not complete, showing only those names and relationships mentioned in the book. John Halse of Kenedon is thought to have had 36 children by two wives. With so many called Richard, and various spellings of Halse, there is bound to be some confusion in the records. The relationships above are therefore frequently taken from deeds and sales recorded in the National Archives, full details given in Notes . My humble thanks goes to the incredible work of John Young on ancestry.com, who seems to have most successfully pieced together the Halse family records. John sadly died in 2004.

The Grenville Family*

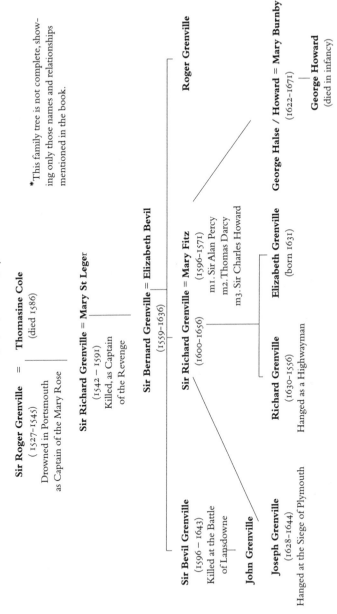

*This family tree is not complete, showing only those names and relationships mentioned in the book.

Sir Roger Grenville = **Thomasine Cole**
(1527-1545)   (died 1586)
Drowned in Portsmouth
as Captain of the Mary Rose

Sir Richard Grenville = **Mary St Leger**
(1542 – 1591)
Killed, as Captain
of the Revenge

Sir Bernard Grenville = **Elizabeth Bevil**
(1559-1636)

Sir Richard Grenville = **Mary Fitz**
(1600-1656)   (1596-1571)
                   m1. Sir Alan Percy
                   m2. Thomas Darcy
                   m3. Sir Charles Howard

Roger Grenville

George Halse / Howard = **Mary Burnby**
(1622-1671)

George Howard
(died in infancy)

Sir Bevil Grenville
(1596 – 1643)
Killed at the Battle
of Lansdowne

John Grenville

Joseph Grenville
(1628-1644)
Hanged at the Siege of Plymouth

Richard Grenville
(1630-1556)
Hanged as a Highwayman

Elizabeth Grenville
(born 1631)

The Howard Family of Saffron Walden*

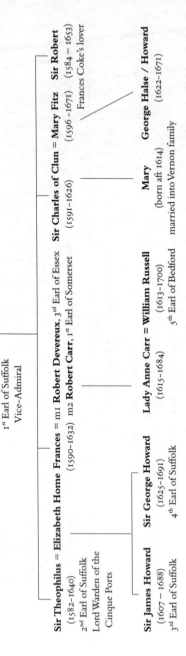

Sir Thomas Howard = **Katherine Knyvet** of Charleton
(1561 – 1626)   (1563 – 1638)
1ˢᵗ Earl of Suffolk
Vice-Admiral

Sir Theophilus = **Elizabeth Home**   **Frances** = m1 **Robert Devereux**, 3ʳᵈ Earl of Essex   **Sir Charles of Clun** = **Mary Fitz**   **Sir Robert**
(1582-1640)   (1590-1632) m2 **Robert Carr**, 1ˢᵗ Earl of Somerset   (1591-1626)   (1596-1671)   (1584 – 1653)
2ⁿᵈ Earl of Suffolk   Frances Coke's lover
Lord Warden of the
Cinque Ports

Sir James Howard   **Sir George Howard**   **Lady Anne Carr** = **William Russell**   **Mary**   **George Halse / Howard**
(1607 – 1688)   (1625-1691)   (1615-1684)   (1613-1700)   (born aft 1614)   (1622-1671)
3ʳᵈ Earl of Suffolk   4ᵗʰ Earl of Suffolk   5ᵗʰ Earl of Bedford   married into Vernon family

*This family tree is not complete; it is very much simplified to show only those names and relationships mentioned in the book. For full details of the Howard family tree, I recommend amongst others: www.wikipedia.org

References

BOOKS

Alford, Revd D.P., *The Abbots of Tavistock* (W. Brendon & Son, 1891)

Baring-Gould, S., *Devonshire Characters and Strange Events*, (The Bodley Head, 1908)

Bray, Mrs A.E., *Traditions, Legends, Superstitions, and Sketches of Devonshire on the Borders of the Tamar and the Tavy*, (J. Murray, 1836)

Cook, K., *Whitchurch Parish* (Tavistock and District Local History Society, 2002)

Dacre, M., *Devonshire Folk Tales* (The History Press, 2010)

Davies, S., *Unbridled Spirits - Women of the English Revolution: 1640-1660* (The Women's Press, 1999)

Du Maurier, D., *The King's General* (Victor Gollancz Ltd, 1946)

Edward, J. et al, Dutkanicz D. (ed), *Sinners in the Hands of an Angry God and other Puritan Sermons* (Dover Publications, 2005)

Eliot-Drake, Lady, *The Family and Heirs of Sir Francis Drake*, Volume 1, (Smith Elder & Co, 1911)

Fox, J., *The King's Smuggler: Jane Whorwood, Secret Agent to Charles I* (The History Press, 2010)

Fraser, A., *The Weaker Vessel* (Weidenfeld & Nicolson, 1984)

Gaunt, P., *The Cromwell Gazetteer* (Alan Sutton Publishing, 1987)

Gillespie, K., *Domesticity and Dissent in the Seventeenth Century: English Women's Writing and the Public Sphere* (Cambridge University Press, 2004)

Gowing, L., *Domestic Dangers* in Oxford Studies in Social History, 1996

Gowing, L., *Common Bodies: Women, Touch and Power in Seventeenth Century England* (Yale University Press, 2003)

Greeves, Dr T., 'The Great Courts or Parliaments of Devon Tinners 1474-1786' in *Transactions of the Devonshire Association, Vol. 119*, pp. 145-167, 1987

Greeves, Dr T., 'Lydford Castle and Its Prison' in *Dartmoor Magazine*, No. 79, pp 8-10, 2005

Heritage House Group, *Powderham Castle* (Heritage House Group Ltd, 2006)

Hill, C., *The World Turned Upside Down* (Penguin Books 1972)

Hodgson-Wright, S., *Women's Writing of the Early Modern Period 1588-1688: An Anthology* (Edinburgh University Press, 2002)

Hynes, K., *Haunted Plymouth* (The History Press, 2010)

Jeffrey, K. (ed), *Audley End* (English Heritage, 1997)

Keble-Chatterton, E., *King's Cutters and Smugglers 1700-1855*, (George Allen & Company, 1912)

McCann, M., *The Wilding* (Faber & Faber, 2010)

Mildren, J., *Castle of Devon* (Bossney Books, 1987)

Miller, A.C, 'Lady Howard and Sir Richard Grenville' in *Report and Transactions of the Devonshire Association,* Volume 101, 1969

Miller, A.C., 'Lady Howard and her Children' in *Report and Transactions of the Devonshire Association,* Volume 102, 1970

Miller, A.C, 'The Impact of the Civil War on Devon and the Decline of the Royalist Cause in the West of England 1644-5' in *Report and Transactions of the Devonshire Association* Volume 104, 1972

Miller, A.C, 'The Puritan Minister John Syms' in *Devon and Cornwall Notes and Queries,* Volume 33.5, 1975

Miller, A.C., *Sir Richard Grenville of the Civil War* (Phillimore and Co, 1979)

Philbrick, N., *Mayflower* (Penguin, 2006)

Photiou, P., *Plymouth's Forgotten War – The Great Rebellion 1642-1646* (Arthur Stockwell, 2005)

Prest, W.R., *The Rise of the Barristers: A Social History of the English Bar 1590-1640* (Clarendon Press, 1991)

Purkiss, D., *The English Civil War: A People's History* (Harper Perennial, 2006)

Radford, G.H., 'Lady Howard of Fitzford' in *Report and Transactions of the Devonshire Association*, Vol. XXII, July pp 66-110, 1890

Radford, R. & U., *The Book of Okehampton* (Halsgrove House, 2002)

Sackville-West, R. *Inheritance – The Story of Knole and the Sackvilles* (Bloomsbury, 2010)

Sackville-West, V., *Knole and the Sackvilles* (National Trust, 1991)

Sansom, C.J. , *Heartstone* (Pan Macmillan, 2010)

Stoyle, M., 'Exeter in the Civil War' in *Devon Archaeology* No. 6 (Devon Archaeological Society, 1995)

Stretton, T., *Women Waging Law in Elizabethan England* (Cambridge University Press, 1998)

Tierney, T., *Cavalier and Puritan Fashions* (Dover Publications, 2005)

Tinniswood, A., *The Verneys* (Jonathan Cape, 2007)

Toynbee, M. & Young, P., *Strangers in Oxford* (Phillimore Press, 1973)

Treece, M., *No More The Sword* (William Sessions Ltd, 2002)

Watson, J.Y., *The Tendring Hundred in the Olden Time: A Series of Sketches* (Kessinger Publishing, 2008)

White, P., *Classic Devon Ghost Stories* (Tor Mark Press, 1996)

Woodcock, G., *Tavistock's Yesterdays: Episodes from Her History*, Volume 1, (Tavistock District and Local History Society 1985)

Woodcock, G., *Tavistock: A History* (Phillimore & Co., 2008)

ORIGINAL DOCUMENTS

Held at Devon Record Office

From the Courtenay Papers, from London (L1508M) and
  Devon (D1508M)★

D1508M/Moger/388 Conveyance of Walreddon Manor and
  other properties from Richard Hals and his wife Anna, to
  Sir Francis Glanville and Edward Skitrett (Skirrett?), 1623

D1508M/Moger/399 Quitclaim by Richard Hals of
  Kennadon to John Macy, Yeoman, of all his right in the
  manor of Walreddon and related properties, 21 June 1625

L1508M/E/Legal/Court and Estate papers/39 Petition of
  Edward Courtenay to the privy Council *re* Sir Richard
  Grenville, dated 8 November 1630, with copy warrant
  issued 17 December 1630

D1508M/Moger/436 Indenture by Dame Mary Greenville,
  confirming the conveyance of Walreddon manor and
  other properties to George Cutteford and his sons, noting
  the original conveyance document of 30 October 1627.
  Indenture drawn up on 28 July 1632

L1508M/Family/Testamentary Papers/3 Inquest into the
  death of Francis Courtenay esq, 3 October 1639

D1508M/Moger/393 Writ of custodians of the liberties of
  England to Sheriff of Devon, declaring Mary Howard an
  outlaw because of outstanding debts, and ordering the Sheriff
  to seize any goods of Mary Howard, 23 November 1640

2741 M/T/1 Deed poll of Dame Mary Grenville, widow,
  conveying her property as listed to her son, George
  Howard, 9 January 1661

D1508m/E/Accounts/v/29 Account Book of Lady Elizabeth
  Amerideth, guardian of Sir William Courtenay

D1508M/Moger/434 Indenture between Grace Cutteford of St
  Thomas, Exeter, and Dame Mary Grenville of Fitzford, 6 April 1665

D1508M-11/F/1 Will of Dame Mary Grenville of Fitzford,
  including bequests to her daughters, on condition they
  allow Sir William Courtenay peaceable enjoyment of all
  her lands, 14 October 1671

D1508M-11/F/2 Notice that Sir William Courtenay has
  taken possession of properties at Tavistock, Whitchurch,
  and Bere Ferris. 25 October 1671

★The reference numbers above are from the online records
of the National Archives http://www.nationalarchives.gov.
uk, although I have noticed small discrepancies between
these online references and the paper-based catalogues held
in Devon Record Office. If accessing these files, it is best to
check the reference numbers in the paper-based catalogues
before making document requests.

Held at East Sussex Record Office

SAS/G23/2 Counterpart lease for Berwick and other estates,
  issued by Edward Sackville and witnessed by Thomas
  Robinson, 26 November 1611
SAS/G23/5 Settlement over the manor of Berwick and other
  lands, between various parties including Edward Sackville
  and Thomas Robinson, 23 July 1618
SAS/G23/34 Detailed valuation of the manor of Berwick,
  including surveys by Thomas Robinson, servant of Edward
  Sackville, 1625

Held at National Archives, London

PROB 11/65 The will of William Cuttiford of Plymouth,
  15 February 1581
STAC 8/230/27 Pearse v Hals and Cutteford, 1614
C10/465/61 Cutteford v Grenville in the Court of Chancery,
  1658
PROB 11/285 The will of George Cutteford the younger,
  originally written 13 April 1646, and affirmed at
  Canterbury, as required by the Interregnum administration
  on 8 December 1658

Held at Plymouth and West Devon Record Office

107/85c Admission of Arthur Perryman and family to an eighth
  part of Rodgparke, 8 acres, late of Richard Halse, gentleman,

and Jerome and John, his sons, 11 September 1615

1/642/67 Letters and papers of Henry Rexford of Plymouth, from 1639 to 1653, including a letter from George Howard, *c.* 1651

Held at West Sussex Record Office

Add Ms 18008 -771 Indenture conveying the farm of Tuddybrook from John Furlong to George Cutteford the younger, student at Exeter College Oxford, signed by John Furlong, 13 January 1628

Add Ms 18008-786 Indenture conveying Walreddon Manor from Richard Hals to John Macy, signed by 'Richard Hals', 20 April 1625

SAS-WH/49 Copy of Charter of Sackville College in East Grinstead, 8 Jul 1632

Add Ms 18008-818 A petition from George Cutteford the elder, a prisoner, to the King, with a response by King Charles I and notes from Sir John Berkeley, and signed by Sir John Berkeley, 25 September 1644

Add Ms 18008-825 Inventory of the goods and debts of George Cutteford the elder, who died on 16 April 1645, taken at the time of death of his son George Cutteford. Inventory taken by John Macy, Thomas Willy and William Spry, on 3 September 1646

Add Ms 18008 John Cutteford's papers, held in the Sackville Collection, including commissions appointing John Cutteford to the office of 'wayter and searcher' for the port of Bristol 1656 – 1662

Add Ms 18008-826 'A note of what my mother owes me and what I have paid out for her' - Letter from John Cutteford, detailing his accounts, *c.* 1660 but undated

ONLINE RESOURCES

Although I have referred to original documents where possible during the research for this book, I am indebted to the writers and contributors for the following websites and online resources:

www.ancestry.co.uk

www.battlefieldstrust.com

www.british-civil-wars.co.uk

www.british-history.ac.uk, including the following references:

Monger, R.F. & Penfold, P.A., (eds). 'Acts of the Privy Council of England', vol. 45 1629-30 (1960)

Penfold, P.A. (ed), 'Acts of the Privy Council of England' , vol. 46 1630-31 (1964)

'Confession of James Coutrenay of his knowledge or participation in various robberies of cloth, church jewles, fishing nets, cattle etc, at various times'. From 'Henry VIII: August 1538 1-5' Letters and papers, Foreign and Domestic, Henry VIII, vol. 13, Part 2 August-December 1538. (1893)

Nicholas Hals to Sir Robert Cecil. 17 May 1595, 'Answer to the complaint against him of Mr Watts, alderman of London, for obtaining certain conchinella and indico out of Watts's ship the Jewel'. Endorsed: 17 May, 1595. From: 'Cecil Papers: May 1595, 16-31' Calendar of the Cecil Papers in Hatfield House, vol. 5. 1594-95 pp. 207-25 (1894)

http://centres.exeter.ac.uk

www.dartmooronline.co.uk

www.devonheritage.org

www.devonperspectives.co.uk

http://english-civil-war-society.org.uk

www.english-heritage.org.uk

www.legendarydartmoor.co.uk

www.middletemple.org.uk

www.nationalarchives.gov.uk

www.nationaltrust.org.

www.powderham.co.uk

www.shadyoldlady.com

http://smugglers.oldcornwall.org

www.thepeerage.com

www.tudorplace.com.ar

http://uk-genealogy.org.uk

www.wikipedia.org

Other titles published by The History Press

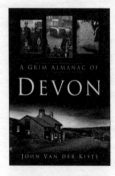

A Grim Almanac of Devon

JOHN VAN DER KISTE

The history of Devon is full of dark deeds and horrible happenings. Among the county's claims to fame are England's first documented serial killer, Robert de Middlecote, the murderous monk, ; and the saga of John 'Babbacombe Lee', the convicted killer who in 1885 became the 'man they could not hang'.

978 0 7509 5047 3

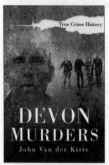

Devon Murders

JOHN VAN DER KISTE

This volume recounts several notable cases, from the killing of Sarah and Edward Glass at Wadland Down in 1827, to the horrific murder of Emma Doidge and her boyfriend William Rowe, by Peter Tavey in 1892, and the triple murder of Emily Maye and her daughters at West Charleton, Kingsbridge, in 1936, which remains unsolved to this day.

978 0 7509 4408 3

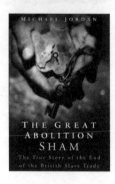

The Great Abolition Sham

MICHAEL JORDAN

Seventeenth-century Britain was built on the back of the slave trade but few of the people who profited from this thought about the lost lives behind their luxuries. By the eighteenth century things were different, people began to question whether anyone had the right to buy and sell another human being, and so the Abolition Movement was born. This book reveals the truth behind the abolition story.

978 0 7524 3491 6

Visit our website and discover thousands of other History Press books.

www.thehistorypress.co.uk